About the Author and Photograph

Vince Burton

From childhood I have always had a strong fascination with nature. When I was given my first camera it was no surprise I focussed it on wildlife. I wanted to capture the beauty in nature and to travel the world in doing so.

I have been very privileged in my life so far to visit a great number of exotic places in search of some amazing wildlife. In Borneo I spent time with one of our closest relations, orangutans and learnt of the threat to their survival as palm oil plantations replace their forest home.

Staying in tents in the Maasai Mara I was on hand to observe many amazing wildlife events. Just like on the 'Big Cat Diary' I observed the natural behaviour of several individuals and witnessed their daily struggles to survive.

Having witnessed this, and so much more, I have seen how our desire for wealth and resources is forcing nature into ever smaller pockets of natural environments, or 'nature reserves', to survive in. This has led me towards wanting to use my images to help educate and inspire people to preserve the amazing natural world that we are so rapidly destroying.

In addition to this book, more of my images can be found on my website at; vbphotography.co.uk.

About the Contributing Photographer

<u>Paul Sawer</u>

I first met Paul on a photography trip to Kenya and we have been close friends ever since, sharing a number of wildlife expeditions.

Paul was brought up on the doorstep of the famous RSPB Minsmere nature reserve so it's no surprise he gained a passion for natural history at an early age. Later he followed his interest in photography where he sought to record the wildlife as he observed it, whilst attempting to emulate the images of top photographers of that time.

Initially disappointed with his results, he set out to develop techniques that would bring the subject not only within range, but also to the exact position required for each shot. Eventually this approach led to success and him achieving the results he desired.

Paul followed his dream and turned professional in 2018, using his knowledge of wildlife and photography to guide others in a number of UK workshops and several trips overseas.

Paul has contributed approximately a quarter of the images in this book and more of his work can be found on his website at; www.paulsawer.co.uk.

365 Days in Nature

Author and photographer Vince Burton
also featuring images by Paul Sawer

365 Days in Nature

Olympia Publishers
London

www.olympiapublishers.com
OLYMPIA PAPERBACK EDITION

A CIP catalogue record for this title is available from the British Library.

ISBN: 978-1-78830-761-1

First Published in 2020

Olympia Publishers
Tallis House
2 Tallis Street
London
EC4Y 0AB

Printed in Great Britain

Acknowledgements

Firstly, thank you to my fellow photographer and close friend Paul who contributed many images to this book. Without him this project would have taken me several more years to complete.

Also, a huge thank you to the professional photographers whose hides I have visited to obtain a number of the images featured in this book;
www.scottishphotographyhides.co.uk
wildlife-photography-hides.co.uk
aviemoreospreys.co.uk
neilmcintyre.com
mullcharters.com
andyhoward.co.uk
gjwp.co.uk

And last, but by no means least, a huge thank you to my wife, Monika, for her support, for putting up with my early morning wake up calls and never being around to complete the jobs around the house I was supposed to.

Foreword

When I initially came up with the concept of this book I thought it would be easy to find enough images within my portfolio to fill every page. In reality however, after a search of my archives, I was far from my target. Whilst I could have easily filled the pages with repeat subjects, such as kingfishers, deer and owls with a few record shots of other species, my objective was not only to have a quality image for every day of the year but to also have a good variety of species. I called upon my close friend Paul Sawer to include further photographs but even then we still came up short, resulting in our continuing to collect imagery for a further three years. The result is a body of work that illustrates the UK's huge variety of wildlife and some of the best times of year to enjoy them.

Kingfisher (Alcedo atthis)   *500mm f4 1/2000 ISO1250*

This is one of the UK's most brilliantly coloured birds. Not much larger than a sparrow, the deep orange underparts contrast beautifully with the greenish blue of the folded wings. A kingfisher has a second, almost indescribable electric blue. It's this blue along its back which is often your first sight of this bird as it flashes like lightning away down the river.

Turnstone (Arenaria interpres)   *320mm f5.6 1/500 ISO400*

In photography the 'golden hour' or 'magic hour' is the first hour after sunrise and the last hour before sunset. These two hours provide a different kind of light which can enhance an image. The light is more diffused, less intense and gives a warm glow to the subject. Above is an image of a turnstone doing exactly as its name suggests, taken during the last light of day, before sunset.

1 2 3 4 5 6 7 8 9 10 11 12 13 14 15 16 17 18 19 20 21 22 23 24 25 26 27 28 29 30 31

JAN

Red squirrel (Sciurus vulgaris)   *214mm f5 1/200 ISO2500*

Red squirrels don't hibernate, instead they bury any leftover food in holes or crevices to be eaten when food is scarce. This means that winter can be a great season to photograph them as they spend time on the floor, looking for additional fallen food or trying to remember where they buried a snack.

Crested tit (Lophophanes cristatus)   *500mm f4 1/500 ISO2000*

A great wildlife image is not just about capturing the subject, but is also about capturing the environment in which it lives. The crested tit has a restricted range in the UK, only being found in the great Caledonian pine forests of Scotland.

1 2 3 4 5 6 7 8 9 10 11 12 13 14 15 16 17 18 19 20 21 22 23 24 25 26 27 28 29 30 31

JAN

Barn owl (Tyto alba)   *24mm f6.3 15secs ISO1600*

The barn owl is an iconic species in the UK; and they're the most widespread of all owl species, found on every continent, except Antarctica. I call this image 'The Hunter', it was taken using a combination of flash and a longer exposure to capture the sky.

Otter (Lutra lutra)   *400mm f5.6 1/200 ISO1000*

Otters are predominantly nocturnal in freshwater rivers and lakes, so what a great way to photograph one, at night, during its fishing activity. This arrangement required four flashes to be set up around the pond, two at the front and two at the back to provide even lighting.

Grey seal (Halichoerus grypus)   *340mm f5.6 1/500 ISO200*

Norfolk has one of the largest grey seal populations in the UK. Other hotspots on the east coast include Lincolnshire and Northumbria. In total it's estimated that 40% of the world's grey seal population lives around the UK shores.

Herring gull (Larus argentatus)   *330mm f6.3 1/3200 ISO2500*

A scenic shot, almost a landscape image. This shows the herring gull in its environment against the crashing waves.

1 2 3 4 5 6 7 8 9 10 11 12 13 14 15 16 17 18 19 20 21 22 23 24 25 26 27 28 29 30 31

JAN

Another example of showing the subject in its environment. Not every image has to be a frame filler.

In my opinion, it's nice to show where the subject lives, by including a bit of its habitat, such as this Caledonian pine.

Crested tit (Lophophanes cristatus)   *500mm f5 1/320 ISO3200*

Red squirrel (Sciurus vulgaris)   *45mm f8 1/200 ISO 2500*

A great wildlife image is not just about capturing the subject, but is also about capturing the personality of the subject and telling its story. This image shows what great subjects squirrels can be, and their cheeky personality as this one plays peek-a-boo from behind the tree.

Otter (Lutra lutra)   *168mm f5.6 1/500 ISO1250*

As mentioned earlier otters are predominantly nocturnal in freshwater rivers and lakes, and therefore very difficult to see, let alone photograph. However, during harsh cold winters when food is scarce, you may catch glimpses of them during daylight hours. This one however was more interested in rolling in the snow.

Grey seal (Halichoerus grypus) *35mm f7.1 1/640 ISO250*

The scientific name, "Halichoerus grypus" comes from the Greek for "hooked-nose sea-pig". Grey seal pups are born with white fluffy fur. They are fed on milk containing approx. 60% fat and can quadruple in weight by the time they are weaned at around 21 days. At this point the mother leaves the pup and eventually hunger forces it to sea to feed itself.

Blackbird (Turdus merula)   *600mm f5 1/5000 ISO3200*

Winter can be a great time to get close to all kinds of wildlife. During cold spells and particularly snowfall, food becomes scarce. Offering supplemental food not only benefits the wildlife, but also means you can enjoy observing many different species. However, this can bring conflict between some individuals as they fight over what is available.

JAN   1 2 3 4 5 6 7 8 9 10 11 12 **13** 14 15 16 17 18 19 20 21 22 23 24 25 26 27 28 29 30 31

Hen harrier (Circus cyaneus)   *600mm f4 1/5000 ISO320*

Images taken during snowfall can add a real atmosphere, however it does provide a challenge, as the camera's autofocus may attempt to focus on the falling snowflakes instead of the subject.

1 2 3 4 5 6 7 8 9 10 11 12 13 14 15 16 17 18 19 20 21 22 23 24 25 26 27 28 29 30 31

JAN

Whilst images of static subjects are great, it's always pleasing to photograph your subjects in action. The key to obtaining this type of image is repetition. It will usually take many attempts to get the subject in the right position, the right pose, and sharp where required. Once a subject continues to use the same path, it will often do so in exactly the same way. This means settings and composition can be tweaked to gain the perfect image.

Red squirrel (Sciurus vulgaris)   *500mm f4.5 1/2500 ISO4000*

JAN 1 2 3 4 5 6 7 8 9 10 11 12 13 14 15 16 17 18 19 20 21 22 23 24 25 26 27 28 29 30 31

Red squirrel (Sciurus vulgaris)   *500mm f4 1/400 ISO2000*

Red squirrels have four fingers on each front paw, plus a vestigial thumb, and five toes
on their rear feet. Their double-jointed ankles allow them to go down a tree headfirst.

The red kite is a common site along the roads leading into Wales and also around rubbish dumps, however they are now expanding their range. There is a pair near me in Norfolk and it's great to see them soaring high in the sky.

Red kite (Milvus milvus)   *400mm f8 1/1250 ISO640*

Mountain hare (Lepus timidus)   *500mm f5 1/500 ISO1600*

Mountain hares change their colour in winter from dappled shades of brown to white, which keeps them camouflaged against the snow. However in winters when the snowfall is late or doesn't arrive at all, the hares will stand out and will therefore have to spend much more time trying to hide from predators.

Snow bunting (Plectrophenax nivalis)   *600mm f6.3 1/4000 ISO3200*

This charming winter visitor to the south must be one of the hardiest songbirds, as well as one of my favourites. Yet despite its attractive white patterned plumage, flocks of these birds can still be very difficult to spot, blending into their beach, shingle or salt-marsh surroundings. From late September to February birds winter along the east coast of the UK as far south as Kent and can be found on beaches searching for seeds and insects.

Mute swan (Cygnus olor)   *600mm f8 1/2500 ISO250*

These elegant looking birds grow up to 1.6 metres long and have a wingspan that is over 2 metres wide. This makes them the largest bird in Britain. Mute swans mate for life and may use the same nest every year. Their nest is a large mound of vegetation in shallow water or on land, close to the edge of a lake or river.

1 2 3 4 5 6 7 8 9 10 11 12 13 14 15 16 17 18 19 20 21 22 23 24 25 26 27 28 29 30 31

JAN

Shoveler (Anas clypeata)   *300mm f5.6 1/400 ISO400*

I'm not usually a fan of close ups or head shots. However sometimes they can serve a purpose, to show small detail. At around 7cm long, the bill of the shoveler is longer than the head itself (try it!). The series of comb-like bristles shown here are called lamellae and act very similar to the baleen plates of a whale in filtering food from the water.

Shelduck (Tadorna tadorna)   *600mm f9 1/6400 ISO1250*

The shelduck is one of our largest ducks, growing as big as some geese. It's mainly found in coastal areas, feeding on small invertebrates that it finds in the mud of estuaries and sandy beaches. It has spread inland, as flooded gravel pits with sandy shores and gravel banks provide a perfect feeding ground.

Common buzzard (Buteo buteo)   *600mm f5 1/4000 ISO2500*

As its name suggests, this is the commonest and most widespread bird of prey in the UK. Buzzards are variable in colour, with some dark brown all over to paler variations. All birds have dark wingtips and a finely barred tail. Their wings are rounded and the tail is often fanned.

Red fox (Vulpes vulpes)   *28mm f8 20secs ISO1000*

Foxes are often nocturnal and also very unpredictable. This is an image I had sought for ages, a wide angle shot of a fox doing its nightly rounds, whilst capturing the night sky above it. The foxes in urban areas are often bolder and therefore easier to capture than their shy country cousins.

Grey heron (Ardea cinerea)   *286mm f5.6 1/250 ISO1000*

Until recently I was unaware that grey herons also fished during the night. During the breeding season, it has been suggested that they can fish for up to twenty-three hours a day. This set up utilised four flashes to balance the light, at the front and back of the heron.

Grey heron (Ardea cinerea)   *286mm f5.6 1/250 ISO1000*

Similar to the previous image, only this time the flashes at the front were switched off, so the heron was only lit from behind, creating the rim-light effect.

Red kite (Milvus milvus)   *375mm f5.6 1/5000 ISO400*

The red kite was persecuted to extinction in England and Scotland with only a few pairs clutching to existence in the Welsh valleys. In the late 1980s a reintroduction programme was started at a number of sites, and it remains one of the most successful reintroductions to date. Feeding stations were set up at several locations in the UK and have become a great place to photograph these magnificent birds, one of the best known being at Gigrin Farm in Wales where hundreds of birds can gather for a helpful hand out.

1 2 3 4 5 6 7 8 9 10 11 12 13 14 15 16 17 18 19 20 21 22 23 24 25 26 **27** 28 29 30 31

JAN

Harvest mouse (Micromys minutus)   *100mm f18 1/160 ISO200*

As a photographer it's always useful to try different things and come up with new ideas. This is an alternative to shooting in the wild, photographing in a studio where everything, including the wildlife can be controlled. This was an idea for an image I had been waiting to shoot, a silhouette of a mouse on an ear of wheat.

Red fox (Vulpes vulpes) and pheasant (Phasianus colchicus)   *200mm f5.6 1/1250 ISO400*

Just as night follows day, death stalks life with the same indifference. For a predator, prey firstly has to be identified as such and then it has to be caught. Prey has developed different methods to avoid capture, thus the predator-prey interaction becomes something akin to an evolutionary arms race.

Snow bunting (Plectrophenax nivalis)   *500mm f5.6 1/3200 ISO250*

This could be a resident bird of the Cairngorms, as around 60 pairs are believed to breed there in the summer. During the winter the number in the UK explodes as birds migrate from the colder north and populate the east coast of the UK.

1 2 3 4 5 6 7 8 9 10 11 12 13 14 15 16 17 18 19 20 21 22 23 24 25 26 27 28 29 30 31

JAN

Long-tailed tits are early nesters. They also have one of the highest nest failure rates. If a nest does fail, rather than try again they will often help to rear nestlings of other birds that formed part of their winter flock, to whom they may be related. Researchers have also found a failed breeding long-tailed tit helping to raise an adjacent brood of great tits.

Long-tailed tits (Aegithalos caudatus)   155mm f11 1/250 ISO200

Kingfisher (Alcedo atthis)   *170mm f5.6 1/8000 ISO2000*

An idea I had over three years before conditions were right to capture a kingfisher diving through a hole in the ice. With winters becoming milder in the UK, I had to be patient to achieve this image.

This is part of a local project. I wanted to achieve an image of a barn owl at night, doing exactly what a barn owl does naturally. This meant photographing my subject in the pitch black with low powered flashes and soft boxes.

Barn owl (Tyto alba)   *70mm f8 1/200 ISO800*

1 2 3 4 5 6 7 8 9 10 11 12 13 14 15 16 17 18 19 20 21 22 23 24 25 26 27 28

Brown hare (Lepus europaeus)   *600mm f4 1/160 ISO400*

Famous for their boxing skills, they may look like large gentle rabbits but brown hares are actually powerful athletes that can reach speeds of up to 40mph. This hare doesn't have boxing on its mind, but is simply trying to keep warm during the freezing conditions.

A continuation of the project with the barn owl. I am often searching for a good reflection shot, whenever the opportunity arises. This was an image I had not seen done before, a barn owl and its reflection, so I started to plan the shot.

Barn owl (Tyto alba)   *100mm f8 1/200 ISO1000*

Common buzzard (Buteo buteo)   *600mm f 5 1/2000 ISO3200*

Common buzzards often feed on carion, especially during the winter months when food can be scarce. This can be an opportunity to entice them to return to a locality on a regular basis.

1 2 3 4 5 6 7 8 9 10 11 12 13 14 15 16 17 18 19 20 21 22 23 24 25 26 27 28

FEB

Tawny owl (Strix aluco)   *55mm f5.6 15secs ISO1250*

This is an example of making a picture with an image. Instead of just photographing the subject close up and filling the frame, I chose to show it in its environment and looking natural. In order to achieve this image, I needed a cloudy night, with the light pollution illuminating the sky.

Starling (Sturnus vulgaris)   *79mm f5.6 1/200 ISO320*

Murmuration refers to the phenomenon that results when hundreds, sometimes thousands, of starlings fly in swooping, intricately coordinated patterns in the sky before roosting. A recent study has shown that starlings pay attention to a fixed number, just seven of their nearest neighbours, to retain flock cohesion, regardless of its density.

Blue tit (Cyanistes caeruleus)   *600mm f5 1/5000 ISO1250*

Here is an example of using props within your image. The snowdrops showing through the snow, allow the possibility of feeding the hungry birds in a certain location to obtain this image.

Mountain hare (Lepus timidus)   *500mm f5.6 1/2500 ISO800*

This has got to be one of the hardiest mammals in the UK. It's also the only native member of their group, with rabbits and brown hares thought to have been introduced by the Normans and Romans respectively. In fact, this is our only truly Arctic mammal restricted to high ground (usually above 300 - 400m).

Sometimes it's nice to try something a little different. This shot was an attempt to gain two subjects within the same shot. As always in the winter, I had been putting out a variety of food. It was interesting to see which species tolerated each other.

Great spotted woodpecker and great tit   *400mm f6.3 1/400 ISO2000*

Turnstone (Arenaria interpres)   *700mm f5.6 1/3200 ISO1250*

Capturing behaviour or the subject in motion can always be a challenge. In this instance, the subject is doing as its name suggests, not just turning the stone but flipping it into the air.

Short-eared owl (Asio flammeus)   *600mm f5.6 1/5000 ISO1600*

And sometimes the subject just wants its picture taken and poses :)

Red squirrel (Sciurus vulgaris)

500mm f6.3 1/1250 ISO800

A red squirrel eating its winter store in the Cairngorms. According to the Forestry Commission's website, squirrels can be left or right handed when they eat a pine cone.

Bullfinch (Pyrrhula pyrrhula)   *400mm f5.6 1/320 ISO2500*

This shot was taken in the early morning light as the sun rises. Shooting into the light rather than with it, can sometimes create some magical effects. As with all rules, sometimes they are there to be broken, and photography is no exception.

Golden eagle (Aquila chrysaetos)   *255mm f5.6 1/800 ISO3200*

Golden eagles mate for life, although if one of the pair dies, the survivors have been known to readily accept a new mate. They tend not to breed until they are at least four or five years old. A survey carried out in 2016 suggested that the golden eagle population has now soared to over 500 breeding pairs, all currently in Scotland.

1 2 3 4 5 6 7 8 9 10 11 12 13 14 15 16 17 18 19 20 21 22 23 24 25 26 27 28   FEB

This impressive bird of prey is the largest and broadest-winged of the harrier family. It's likely spotted flying low over reedbeds and grazing marshes, with the wings raised in the prominent and characteristic 'V' shape.

The courtship of the marsh harrier is a great wildlife spectacle and is a sight to behold. Both birds tumbling through the sky, with their talons locked in mid-air.

Marsh harrier (Circus aeruginosus)   600mm f7.1 1/1600 ISO250

Sparrowhawk (Accipiter nisus)　　　　　　　　　　*500mm f5 1/3200 ISO2000*

Eye to eye with its prey, before it devours it. The female sparrowhawk, being up to 25% larger than the male and up to twice as heavy, is one of the greatest size variations of any bird species. The difference in size between the male and female results in them hunting differently. The male will hunt mainly in woodland, targeting smaller birds such as tits and finches, whereas the female may choose to target slightly larger birds such as starlings and thrushes out in the open.

1 2 3 4 5 6 7 8 9 10 11 12 13 14 15 16 17 18 19 20 21 22 23 24 25 26 27 28

FEB

Water rail (Rallus aquaticus)   *500mm f4.5 1/1600 ISO3200*

This very elusive bird is more often heard than seen. Smaller in size than a moorhen, it feeds on tiny invertebrates.

Water rail (Rallus aquaticus)   *500mm f4.5 1/1000 ISO3200*

This image was taken early one winter's morning as the sun was climbing into the sky, the golden colours reflected in the river.

Brown hare (Lepus europaeus) *600mm f4 1/200 ISO800*

Brown hares were thought to have been introduced to the UK by the Romans. They are now widespread on low ground throughout England, Wales and Scotland. Photographing these subjects can be difficult and often consists of laying on the ground covered in camouflaged netting, or driving around country lanes and shooting from the car.

Whooper swan (Cygnus cygnus)   *600mm f5.6 1/2000 ISO250*

The Icelandic population of whooper swans breed exclusively in Iceland and winter primarily in Britain and Ireland, with smaller numbers remaining in Iceland. Whooper swans undertake what is probably the longest sea crossing of any swan species, migrating 800 - 1,400 km between Britain/Ireland and Iceland.

Goldeneye (Bucephala clangula)　　　　　　　　　*600mm f6.3 1/2500 ISO2500*

The common goldeneye is named for its brilliant yellow iris. This diving duck is one of the earliest birds to breed in the UK and this picture shows a male during his courtship display.

Brown hare (Lepus europaeus)   *600mm f5 1/6400 ISO800*

Hares are a variety of golden-brown colours with a pale belly, white tail and black tips on the ears. This can be seen clearly in this image by setting the hare against a snowy background.

1 2 3 4 5 6 7 8 9 10 11 12 13 14 15 16 17 18 19 20 21 22 **23** 24 25 26 27 28

FEB

Mountain hare (Lepus timidus)   *500mm f5.6 1/1000 ISO800*

With their stunning white winter coats, mountain hares are a sight not to be missed. Unlike brown hares and rabbits, they are native to the UK. During winter days they often rest in 'forms', a small hollow in the ground or snow, in order to keep warm. With care and patience some individuals can be approached slowly while they rest, as moving uses valuable energy. This image has been converted to black and white to show the fur against the snowy background.

Mountain hare (Lepus timidus)   *500mm f5 1/4000 ISO500*

During late February to early March the mountain hares start to become more active. As temperatures rise and the days lengthen, the hare's attention turns to finding a partner. Chasing and boxing can occur, making these great subjects to photograph.

1 2 3 4 5 6 7 8 9 10 11 12 13 14 15 16 17 18 19 20 21 22 23 24 **25** 26 27 28

FEB

Mountain hare (Lepus timidus)

The Three Amigos! Every rule is made to be broken so why should this book be any different. I know there is supposed to be a different photo on every page. However, this image just wasn't done justice on a single page, so instead I've chosen a kind of centre spread.

500mm f8 1/3200 ISO800

These three hares just happened to be sitting close to one another and fortunately almost on the same focal plane. An aperture of f8 was chosen to keep all three reasonably sharp whilst maintaining a decent shutter speed.

1 2 3 4 5 6 7 8 9 10 11 12 13 14 15 16 17 18 19 20 21 22 23 24 25 26 27 28

FEB

Goldfinch (Carduelis carduelis)

500mm f5.6 1/3200 ISO400

Another of the UK's most brilliantly coloured birds, the goldfinch. This bird eats small seeds and has become a regular visitor to people's gardens. Recent surveys suggest that 70% more people see these birds in their garden now than 20 years ago. Niger seed placed in feeders, or as here on dried teasel heads, can provide some excellent photographic opportunities and shows that you don't always have to travel far to find a subject.

FEB 1 2 3 4 5 6 7 8 9 10 11 12 13 14 15 16 17 18 19 20 21 22 23 24 25 26 27 28

Brown hare (Lepus europaeus)　　　　　　　　　*500mm f7.1 1/800 ISO800*

Hares can actually breed from January to October, contrary to the old saying "as mad as a March hare", which is when most people assume they breed. These two certainly had romantic ideas, well at least the male did. It's usually the female hare that starts the boxing, to show the male she is not yet ready for his advances. He will follow her around patiently until she becomes receptive, preventing other males approaching in the meantime.

1 2 3 4 5 6 7 8 9 10 11 12 13 14 15 16 17 18 19 20 21 22 23 24 25 26 27 28 29 30 31　　MA

Sparrowhawk (Accipiter nisus)

500mm f5.6 1/3200 ISO400

This is a male sparrowhawk. Due to the size difference males court the females with caution, and understandably so, as the female can (and sometimes does) kill her suitor.

MAR 1 2 3 4 5 6 7 8 9 10 11 12 13 14 15 16 17 18 19 20 21 22 23 24 25 26 27 28 29 30 31

Crossbill (Loxia curvirostra)   *600mm f6.3 1/1600 ISO3200*

These birds are characterised by the upper and lower beaks crossing at their tips which gives the group its English name. Birds can have beaks that cross to the left or the right and the ratio is approximately 50:50. What determines which way the beak crosses remains a mystery...

Sparrowhawk (Accipiter nisus)　　　　　　　　*500mm f5 1/1250 ISO3200*

As stated previously, the male sparrowhawk, being smaller, is more manoeuvrable and hunts by ambushing small birds in thick woodland. During the breeding season he will provide food for himself, the female (pictured above) and their chicks.

MAR 1 2 3 4 5 6 7 8 9 10 11 12 13 14 15 16 17 18 19 20 21 22 23 24 25 26 27 28 29 30 31

Common frog (Rana temporaria) *280mm f4.5 1/2500 ISO800*

Another example that you don't have to travel far to find wildlife. This image was taken in my back garden as frogs began congregating in the pond to mate. On a damp or wet evening, as temperatures rise above freezing, frogs and toads make their journey to their favourite spawning grounds. I have often been out with a torch on such nights and transported them off the dangerous roads to the safety of their oasis.

1 2 3 4 5 6 7 8 9 10 11 12 13 14 15 16 17 18 19 20 21 22 23 24 25 26 27 28 29 30 31 MAR

Little owl (Athene noctua) *500mm f5.6 1/1000 ISO1000*

The little owl typically hunts worms, beetles, moths, small mammals and birds. Their diet can vary greatly throughout the year. Little owls have fantastic eyesight and are able to hunt in the day and at night. They are especially active from dusk to midnight and at dawn; however, during the breeding season they can hunt throughout the day too.

Stoat (Mustela erminea)   *200mm f5.6 1/1000 ISO2500*

A female stoat rarely has more than one litter of young due to her short lifespan. Stoats breed in the warmer months of May and June, but there is a delayed reaction in the uterus of the female stoat meaning that the embryos don't begin to develop for a number of months. After this time, the baby stoats (kits) are born within a month and she gives birth to a litter of between 5 and 15 kits.

1 2 3 4 5 6 7 8 9 10 11 12 13 14 15 16 17 18 19 20 21 22 23 24 25 26 27 28 29 30 31   MA

Images like this can capture the time of year by making the season easily identifiable as in this case, with the early spring blossom.

Goldfinch (Carduelis carduelis)   *140mm f8 1/250 ISO200*

Common toad (Bufo bufo)   *330mm f13 1/250 ISO3200*

Toads, unlike frogs, can live away from water. They come out at night to feed on insects and burrow into the earth in the daytime. I have a toad living underneath the back doorstep; sometimes it comes into the kitchen, not sure why or what for yet.

Harvest mouse (Micromys minutus)   *400mm f10 1/800 ISO2500*

Harvest mice are the smallest rodents in the UK and our only mammal to have a prehensile tail, able to grasp plant stems as they move through the vegetation. This is a young one, not long out of the nest and exploring its surroundings, in this case a daffodil.

Barn owl (Tyto alba)   *45mm f8 1/250 ISO1600*

Again this image is all about timing. The advantage with owls is that they are relatively slow flyers and therefore slightly easier to catch in flight, or landing as in this case. The trick here was to pre-focus on the stump rather than attempting to follow the bird in flight.

I planted this magnolia tree when I first moved into my house. Who would have thought that some twenty years later, a pair of goldfinches would choose to nest in it. This just shows that if you give wildlife a home, it will come. I am lucky enough to be able to photograph this pair from my bedroom window, using the curtains as a hide and the camera shutter on single shot and silent modes.

Goldfinch (Carduelis carduelis)   *500mm f4.5 1/640 ISO500*

Redpoll (Carduelis flammea) — *500mm f5 1/800 ISO80*

People often suggest winter is a quiet time for wildlife with not much happening. However, it does provide an opportunity to photograph different subjects as migrants appear, especially if you tempt them with a nice perch and some food.

Kingfisher (Alcedo atthis)

500mm f5 1/80 ISO500

This image shows one of the reasons why you should still go out in the rain, because you can be creative. Slowing the shutter speed will create streaks of rain, rather than just specks as faster shutter speeds do. I usually start at 1/100th of a second and work down from there.

Greylag goose (Anser anser) *600mm f4 1/2500 ISO2000*

Their name "greylag" is derived from the fact that they are the last goose species to migrate and each year they "lag" behind the other geese. This shot shows the unusual patterns and detail of the wings.

Stoat (Mustela erminea)

500mm f5.6 1/2500 ISO1250

This was a prime example of always being ready. Only a few minutes earlier, a female sparrowhawk had been sitting on this stump, only to be replaced by a predator of a different kind. This stoat in the Scottish Highlands was looking for scraps of meat left behind, whilst trying not to become the next scrap of meat itself.

Nuthatch (Sitta europaea)   *500mm f5 1/250 ISO2000*

Again, this is one of my favourite kinds of images, truly showing the subject in its environment, rather than just a close up or a portrait. With cameras improving all the time and larger lenses becoming more affordable, it's easy to fall into the trap of taking only frame filling pictures of the subject. To me, this kind of image says so much more about the subject.

1 2 3 4 5 6 7 8 9 10 11 12 13 14 15 16 17 18 19 20 21 22 23 24 25 26 27 28 29 30 31   MAF

During periods of snow cover voles and shrews stay underneath the snow. Although mice may move above it, they will spend an increased proportion of time underground eating stored food. When snow cover is more than about 70mm deep and/or frozen the owls will face great difficulty finding and catching food. This can lead to starvation during particularly harsh winters and a decline in the owl population.

Barn owl (Tyto alba)   *70mm f5 1/250 ISO 1600*

Spoonbill (Platalea leucorodia)   *500mm f6.3 1/2500 ISO200*

An image with a difference, showing the eye in sharp focus, but also the attributes of the subject and how it gets its name. In addition, the angle of the bill creates a great lead in diagonal to the point in focus.

This is always a great image to get, showing the interaction between a mother and its young. It also provides a sense of scale to show just how small the young one is.

Brown hare (Lepus europaeus)   *600mm f4 1/640 ISO3200*

Brown hare (Lepus europaeus) *200mm f11 1/640 ISO320*

As with all photography of young and nests, care must be taken not to scare the parents off and result in the young starving or freezing to death. If I am ever fortunate enough to find a subject like this, I only stay for a short while and leave quietly in order to allow the parents to return and look after their precious young.

Kingfisher (Alcedo atthis)   *500mm f5 1/400 ISO800*

It's always nice to show something to reflect the time of year when an image was captured. This kingfisher shot shows the early spring buds of the pussy willow.

Goldeneye (Bucephala clangula)

300mm f5.6 1/2500 ISO400

Ducks are great subjects, one which can be photographed all year round. This image is all about the timing, an attempt to capture the moment this goldeneye dives, with the eye still showing just above the surface. Such pursuit of a particular image can result in hours being lost.

Barn owl (Tyto alba)   *125mm f8 1/250 ISO1600*

Here is a shot of the beautiful barn owl in flight. Barn owls have primary feathers which are serrated like a comb. This allows the breakdown of turbulence into smaller currents called micro-turbulences. The edge of the feather muffles the sound of air flowing over the wing and shifts the angle at which air flows. These soft feathers allow air to pass through, which almost eliminates the sound all together.

Marsh harrier (Circus aeruginosus)   *840mm f5.6 1/2000 ISO200*

The marsh harrier is one of the great success stories in Norfolk. In the early 19th century they were abundant throughout East Anglia. However, by the latter part of the century they had become almost extinct in the UK through habitat loss and persecution. Marsh harriers bred sporadically in the Broads from 1927 to 1975. Since then the number of nests in the county has risen steadily. Today more than 100 females nest in Norfolk each year.

Skylark (Alauda arvensis)

700mm f5.6 1/3200 ISO1000

Only the nightingale rivals the skylark's reputation as one of the finest songsters in the bird world. The skylark's song is fast, complex and highly variable, but (unlike the nightingale's) it's delivered within a narrow frequency range. There can be anything from 160 to over 460 syllables in the song.

Long-tailed tit (Aegithalos caudatus)   *360mm f9 1/6400 ISO4000*

Long-tailed tits build one of the most intricate nests of the bird world. The outside of the doom is constructed of moss, lichen and cobwebs to give it elasticity as the chicks grow whilst the inside can be lined with up to 2,000 feathers to keep it soft and warm.

1 2 3 4 5 6 7 8 9 10 11 12 13 14 15 16 17 18 19 20 21 22 23 24 25 26 27 28 29 30 31

MAR

In spring, the courting great crested grebes put on a spectacular display on lakes, reservoirs and gravel pits over most of the UK.

The climax of the ritual is the weed dance in which both birds, holding tufts of water weed in their bills, paddle furiously to maintain an upright position chest to chest. An unforgettable sight and an impressive display of stamina.

Great crested grebe (Podiceps cristatus)600mm f4 1/2000 ISO800

MAR 1 2 3 4 5 6 7 8 9 10 11 12 13 14 15 16 17 18 19 20 21 22 23 24 25 26 27 28 29 30 31

Brown hare (Lepus europaeus)   *600mm f6.3 1/5000 ISO3200*

The brown hare is Britain's fastest land mammal, reaching speeds of up to 40mph. That makes this kind of image difficult to obtain, capturing the hare in mid leap, with all four feet off the ground.

Dipper (Cinclus cinclus)

500mm f5 1/2500 ISO400

This is an example of a 'low key' image. With the subject out in the bright light, and the background in the shade, it was possible to under expose the image and create an almost black background.

Tawny owl (Strix aluco)   *24mm f14 1/200 ISO400*

A tawny owl in flight. This image required exact timing as the owl flew between two posts and used flash to freeze the motion.

Like other birds, owls cannot chew their food. Small prey are swallowed whole and several hours later the indigestible parts are compressed into a pellet. As the stored pellet partially blocks the owl's digestive system, new prey cannot be swallowed until it's ejected. Regurgitation often signals that an owl is ready to hunt again.

This image was a result of a lengthy project to photograph wild owls after dark. On this particular night, as with several others, the rain was heavy and I was surprised to find the owl out hunting.

Lighting the owl from behind, gives the subject a rim lit effect, whilst also catching the rain adding to the atmosphere of the image.

Barn owl (Tyto alba)　　　*155mm f9 1/200 ISO1000*

Tawny owl (Strix aluco)   *155mm f5.6 1/60 ISO1000*

Another image from my project of photographing wild owls after dark, this time a tawny owl. The use of flash photography to light the subject created a pitch black background. This is how many people would imagine seeing this beautiful nocturnal bird if they were lucky enough to shine a light onto one.

APR

Sparrowhawk (Accipiter nisus)

500mm f4 1/800 ISO2500

The male sparrowhawk, a beautiful bird of prey, but also a deadly assassin. This bird can often invite itself into your garden where it will sit and watch your bird table in the hope of ambushing smaller birds.

Siskin (Carduelis spinus)   *500mm f4 1/1000 ISO2000*

A clean background is often the most pleasing for wildlife images as busy backgrounds tend to distract from the subject. If you are setting something up in your garden, try to ensure the background is a long way from the subject and use a telephoto lens with a shallow depth of field set.

A blue tit collecting a feather for its nest. It's surprising how much behaviour you can observe if you spend time with a subject. As this image shows, you don't have to be in some far away exotic place.

Blue tit (Cyanistes caeruleus)   *260mm f10 1/300 ISO125*

Pheasant (Phasianus colchicus)   *600mm f5 1/2500 ISO250*

Two cock pheasants have a stand off during the mating season. Unfortunately at this time of the year, they only have one thing on their mind, resulting in so many of them getting hit by cars on our roads.

1 2 3 4 5 6 7 8 9 10 11 12 13 14 15 16 17 18 19 20 21 22 23 24 25 26 27 28 29 30   APR

As with most wildlife photography, getting low really does help to separate the subject. The low angle pushes the background further away resulting in a pleasing diffused background, such as this one.

Avocet (Recurvirostra avosetta)   *600mm f7.1 1/8000 ISO1000*

APR   1 2 3 4 5 6 7 8 9 10 11 12 13 14 15 16 17 18 19 20 21 22 23 24 25 26 27 28 29 30

Avocet (Recurvirostra avosetta)   *500mm f5 1/2000 ISO800*

Another example of a low level image. This shot was taken whilst laying flat on the ground with the camera resting on a bean bag rather than a tripod. This places you at eye level with your subject.

As previously mentioned, backgrounds are important in an image. They need to be 'clean' and not too 'busy' in order not to distract from the subject. This image also shows how the colour of the background can complement the subject.

Black redstart (Phoenicurus ochruros)   *600mm f5.6 1/1250 ISO1600*

Harvest mouse (Micromys minutus)   *400mm f6.3 1/2000 ISO2000*

The harvest mouse is the smallest species of rodent in the UK. It can reach between 2.2 to 2.9 inches in length and weighs between 0.14 to 0.39 ounces. This is how it can climb small twigs like the one above without snapping it.

Now a common sight in the countryside, the red-legged partridge is a non-native species. It originated from parts of Europe, including France, hence its other name, the French partridge. This helps to differentiate it from the grey partridge, also known as the English partridge.

Red-legged partridge (Alectoris rufa)   600mm f5.6 1/800 ISO800

APR 1 2 3 4 5 6 7 8 9 10 11 12 13 14 15 16 17 18 19 20 21 22 23 24 25 26 27 28 29 30

Canada goose (Branta canadensis) *500mm f4 1/1250 ISO200*

Canada geese often fly in the very distinctive 'V' formation. As with photographing any bird on the nest, great care needs to be taken not to disturb them or cause them any stress. This is why I use larger lenses on such subjects so that I do not need to get too close. This nest was also on an island, and with myself on the opposite bank, there was an expanse of water between us.

1 2 3 4 5 6 7 8 9 10 11 **12** 13 14 15 16 17 18 19 20 21 22 23 24 25 26 27 28 29 30

APR

Grey heron (Ardea cinerea)   *500mm f5.6 1/250 ISO2000*

This grey heron reacts to another one coming in, making it a more interesting shot than just a bird standing in a field.

Blue tit (Cyanistes caeruleus)   *170mm f16 1/250 ISO100*

This blue tit's collecting nesting material. Again this is something that can easily be set up in your own garden during the nest building season.

Cuckoo (Cuculus canorus) 500mm f5 1/2500 ISO800

Most people know the sound of the cuckoo, and that they lay their eggs in other birds' nests. But did you know that it's only the male bird that makes the 'cuckoo' sound and that the female bird will usually lay her eggs into the nests of the same species that raised her?

Cuckoo (Cuculus canorus)   *500mm f5 1/3200 ISO80*

The cuckoo spends nine months of the year in Africa, only coming to the UK to breed. However, numbers in the UK have declined drastically in recent years and my best views lately have come from Scotland.

It can be fascinating to watch the miracle of how two small birds work tirelessly to produce such a work of art. Long-tailed tits build such a beautiful ball made of moss, lichen and often held together by spiders' webs. They then line the nest with feathers; as many as 2,000 have been counted inside.

Long-tailed tit (Aegithalos caudatus)   *600mm f5.6 1/1600 ISO3200*

Tawny owl (Strix aluco)   *80mm f6.3 1/250 ISO1600*

They say owls don't hunt when it's raining, well some do. This shot was obtained by placing the flashes behind the subject in order to back-light it, and the rain. I have then converted the image to monotone in order to help bring out the raindrops.

When it comes to intelligence ravens rate up there with chimpanzees and dolphins. In captivity they can learn to talk better than some parrots. They can also mimic other noises, such as car engines, other animals and birdcalls.

Raven (Corvus corax)   *500mm f4.5 1/1250 ISO1600*

Goldfinch (Carduelis carduelis)   *500mm f5 1/2500 ISO800*

The prolonged study of a species often reveals unknown secrets. Watching this pair of goldfinches from my window revealed how the male feeds the female by regurgitating seeds whilst she is incubating the eggs, rather than her leaving the nest or the pair sharing incubation duties.

Egyptian goose (Alopochen aegyptiacus)   *300mm f5.6 1/1250 ISO200*

I am always looking for a natural way to frame a subject. This image of a gosling was almost framed perfectly by one of its parents standing in front of it.

Brown hare (Lepus europaeus) *600mm f5.6 1/320 ISO400*

As you may be aware by now, I have always been a fan of low angle shooting. Getting to your subject's eye level provides a different perspective and shows the world as it would appear to them. Brown hares can often be found on rough agricultural land and meadows, but they are also at home on salt-marshes by the coast. This one looks like it's praying, but it's actually cleaning itself.

Lapwing (Vanellus vanellus)   *600mm f5.6 1/800 ISO250*

The bird so nice they named it thrice; green plover, northern lapwing or peewit, after the call it makes. Another example of a low angle shot, this time managing to blur the foreground and the background making the subject stand out by itself.

Hoopoe (Upupa epops)   *700mm f5.6 1/2000 ISO1600*

Unfortunately I cannot tell you where to find hoopoes within the UK. However, some websites and text alerts (such as BirdGuides) can inform you of rare visitors to your local area. There was once a hoopoe spotted for several days in the car park of an Asda supermarket in Suffolk.

1 2 3 4 5 6 7 8 9 10 11 12 13 14 15 16 17 18 19 20 21 22 23 24 25 26 27 28 29 30   APR

Kestrel (Falco tinnunculus)

500mm f5.6 1/3200 ISO3200

Always expect the unexpected! Originally I was shooting the female kestrel on this branch. As I had my face pressed up to the back of the camera, I didn't notice the male fly in and had to quickly re-compose in order to fit both birds in whilst they mated. Unfortunately, I had no time to change to a smaller lens.

Grey heron (Ardea cinerea)   *500mm f7.1 1/640 ISO2500*

If a picture says a thousand words then what does a sequence of shots say? This sequence tells the story of how the heron positions the fish before it can swallow it. Often it's worth using the high-speed shooting mode on the camera and taking a burst during moments of action in order to get the perfect image, or a sequence like this.

Mute swan (Cygnus olor)

55mm f5.6 1/2000 ISO200

Create yourself a project. This is a good way of coming up with great photos of a common subject. I feed this pair of swans through the winter and have done for several years now. As a result, I have earnt their trust and they allow me to share their intimate moments such as this during the breeding season. This has given me the freedom to use a wide angle lens and get in close, rather than having to rely on a hide and a long lens as with other wild subjects.

Mute swan (Cygnus olor)   *32mm f10 25secs ISO2000*

After several years of photographing this pair by day, I thought I would see how they responded to my presence at night. Fortunately they were just as accommodating after dark and I was able to work with them in some longer exposures to show the subject under the stars. The male would often come and sit by my side during these sessions.

As mentioned previously I like to create pictures with my images. In this image I am showing the owl in its environment, a wood carpeted with bluebells. It was taken as the last light of the day filtered through the trees and highlighted the subject.

Tawny owl (Strix aluco)   *145mm f3.2 1/640 ISO400*

APR 1 2 3 4 5 6 7 8 9 10 11 12 13 14 15 16 17 18 19 20 21 22 23 24 25 26 27 28 29 30

Song thrush (Turdus philomelos)   *500mm f5.6 1/800 ISO3200*

Song thrushes used to be a common sight when I was growing up; you would see them as regularly as blackbirds. However, their numbers are now declining. Providing a source of water in your back garden, and in this case moss, can attract rare and unusual visitors.

APR

Every photographer needs to find their own style. In my early days I just wanted to fill the frame with every subject I photographed. Now I look for images that form a picture and, like this image, show the species in its environment.

This image was made possible by knowing the subject. Green woodpeckers love ants and beside this stump was an ants' nest. It was only a matter of time before the woodpecker landed there for some 'fast food'.

Green woodpecker (Picus viridis)   *500mm f6.3 1/400 ISO1600*

Tawny owl (Strix aluco)   *135mm f2.8 1/800 ISO250*

Many will say there is no better sight than a woodland floor carpeted in bluebells. The bluebells flower in early spring, when the chance of frost has reduced, whilst in a race to mature before the leaf canopy above them unfolds and blocks out the majority of the sunlight.

1 2 3 4 5 6 7 8 9 10 11 12 13 14 15 16 17 18 19 20 21 22 23 24 25 26 27 28 29 30 31   MAY

An image of a subject with a clean and simple background sitting on an interesting perch. In this instance the green of the moss and the background combine, making the subject stand out.

Woodpeckers often come to bird feeders to enjoy peanuts. They can also be encouraged onto a perch by drilling holes into it and placing peanuts or fat inside.

Great spotted woodpecker   *500mm f5 1/500 ISO2500*

MAY   1 2 3 4 5 6 7 8 9 10 11 12 13 14 15 16 17 18 19 20 21 22 23 24 25 26 27 28 29 30 31

Red fox (Vulpes vulpes)   *500mm f4.5 1/1000 ISO800*

Foxes are a fantastic subject, but also a very difficult one as they are mainly nocturnal and seek quiet areas. Cemeteries are a good place to see foxes as they are often left undisturbed and can make their dens under gravestones or vegetation in the graveyard. This fox cub is young and has not yet learnt to fear humans. One day it will also grow into its head.

Jackdaw (Corvus monedula)

500mm f6.3 1/2500 ISO3200

Several birds pass food to their mate in order to bond. Kingfishers are probably the best known with their fish pass, but here a pair of jackdaws are participating in the same ritual, just without a fish.

MAY 1 2 3 4 5 6 7 8 9 10 11 12 13 14 15 16 17 18 19 20 21 22 23 24 25 26 27 28 29 30 31

Barn owl (Tyto alba)   *600mm f5.6 1/4000 ISO50*

Photography is often about just capturing a moment. This image shows the instant that this barn owl notices a butterfly coming towards it.

Once known as the golden-crested wren, the goldcrest is Britain's smallest bird, weighing just 5-6g. Despite their tiny size, goldcrests are highly migratory, with a large influx of birds from Scandinavia and the near-continent arriving on the east coast of Britain in the autumn.

Goldcrest (Regulus regulus)   *600mm f8 1/2000 ISO3200*

Adder (Vipera berus)   *700mm f5.6 1/1600 ISO800*

Despite being Britain's only venomous snake, adders are very timid, and only bite in self-defence, usually during attempts to capture or if accidentally stepped on. They have a very distinctive pattern of diamonds on their back and can often be seen basking in warm sun spots. I decided to use a long lens on this one so that I didn't have to get too close.

1 2 3 4 5 6 7 8 9 10 11 12 13 14 15 16 17 18 19 20 21 22 23 24 25 26 27 28 29 30 31   MAY

An example of how different an image appears, just by turning the camera. My first observation is how the subjects appear to be smaller in this image, compared to the image opposite. And yet these were taken from exactly the same spot.

Little owl (Athene noctua)   *500mm f7.1 1/1600 ISO1250*

MAY   1 2 3 4 5 6 7 8 9 10 11 12 13 14 15 16 17 18 19 20 21 22 23 24 25 26 27 28 29 30 31

Little owl (Athene noctua)   *500mm f7.1 1/1600 ISO1250*

This shows that if an image is worth taking in one format, then often it's worth taking in the other format too. Try not to be too rigid when photographing wildlife. Sticking to the same format and the same settings will only result in multiple images looking the same. Try to 'mix it up' a little. Sometimes it won't work, but other times it can create a nice surprise.

A beautiful male sparrowhawk. Attract small birds to an area with either food or water, and predators may soon follow. When I made this reflection pool with a small perch on the side, I expected tits and maybe a robin would sit on it. Imagine my surprise when this bird landed on it. Although it was difficult to lean far enough back inside the hide to fit him and all of his reflection into the shot, whilst also trying not to scare him, the result was well worth the aching back.

Sparrowhawk (Accipiter nisus)   *500mm f7.1 1/320 ISO1000*

MAY   1 2 3 4 5 6 7 8 9 10 11 12 13 14 15 16 17 18 19 20 21 22 23 24 25 26 27 28 29 30 31

Red fox (Vulpes vulpes) *500mm f4.5 1/640 ISO800*

An image of a young fox cub emerging from its den in a cemetery. Foxes often have multiple dens and move between them as food, weather and disturbance dictate. Some dens are in fact never used.

Tawny owl (Strix aluco)

40mm f5.6 1/10 ISO1250

Again as I'm creating a picture with an image, the light and the weather can make such a difference. Look at the same image shot three months earlier on the 6th February and you will see what a difference it can make, even at night.

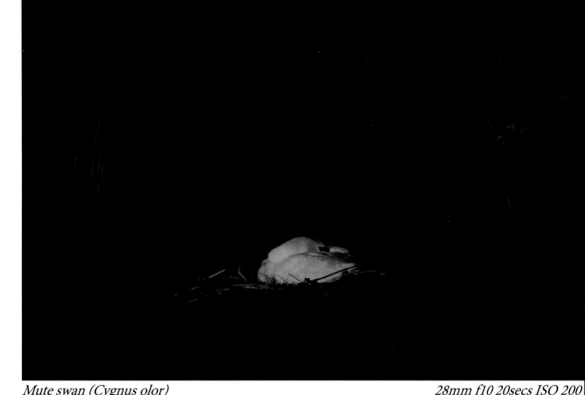

Mute swan (Cygnus olor)   *28mm f10 20secs ISO 200*

This shot was only possible because of the years of work getting this pair relaxed around me. I feed them during the winter months and photograph them in the spring during nesting. After five years they have allowed me to be close to them day or night. This shows just how relaxed the female is as she sleeps on the nest under the stars.

1 2 3 4 5 6 7 8 9 10 11 12 13 14 15 16 17 18 19 20 21 22 23 24 25 26 27 28 29 30 31   MAY

Mute swan (Cygnus olor)   *600mm f8 1/2000 ISO400*

Whilst continuing my project I felt honoured to share some intimate moments like this. As the cygnets began to hatch the mother was on hand to help. With this pair, the male often guarded the nest or indeed sat on the eggs whilst the female was laying one every other day. Once she had finished laying, she took over the parental role and began incubation of the eggs which can take between thirty-six and fourty-two days. As the eggs near hatching, the male again becomes more interested and stays by his mate's side.

MAY 1 2 3 4 5 6 7 8 9 10 11 12 13 14 15 16 17 18 19 20 21 22 23 24 25 26 27 28 29 30 31

Tawny owl (Strix aluco)   *300mm f5.6 1/250 ISO400*

A shot of a tawny owl in woodland where the ground was covered in bluebells. This was taken with a large lens, using a shallow depth of field in order to blur the background, again making the subject stand out.

In winter long-eared owls often roost in groups, which are called 'a parliament of owls'. This owl, unlike the short-eared owl is a nocturnal hunter and a shy bird during the day.

Long-eared owl (Asio otus)   *500mm f4.5 1/5000 ISO800*

Mute swan (Cygnus olor)   *500mm f6.3 1/1600 ISO40*

Spending time with a subject such as this nesting swan allows you to share some special moments. This cygnet has just hatched, with a little help from mum.

It's always good to show a different perspective to your subject. This head on shot provides a chance to show the perfect symmetry with the wings outstretched.

Shelduck (Tadorna tadorna)   *600mm f8 1/6400 ISO1600*

MAY   1 2 3 4 5 6 7 8 9 10 11 12 13 14 15 16 17 18 19 20 21 22 23 24 25 26 27 28 29 30 31

Lapwing (Vanellus vanellus) *600mm f4 1/1000 ISO800*

Male lapwings put on dramatic aerial displays, tumbling through the air, accompanied by their piercing 'peewit' call, which gives them their nickname. Females can be spotted on nests which are simple scrapes in the mud or sand. By late spring, cute, fluffy lapwing chicks such as this one can be seen venturing out to forage.

Long-eared owl (Asio otus)   *500mm f4.5 1/250 ISO2000*

It has been suggested that you can tell the time of day when an owl hunts by the colour of its eyes. Owls with yellow eyes hunt mainly during the day, contrasting with owls which have dark eyes that hunt during the night, and owls with orange eyes that hunt mainly at dusk or dawn. Most owls in the UK are nocturnal and hunt at night but can also be seen hunting at dusk. Some owls, such as the little owl or the short-eared owl, are diurnal, meaning they hunt during the day.

Dipper (Cinclus cinclus)   *700mm f5.6 1/800 ISO1600*

Dippers are often described as the "only truly aquatic songbird" in the UK. They frequent fast-flowing streams and rivers and unlike other birds, they are able to swim, dive, and walk underwater to feed.

1 2 3 4 5 6 7 8 9 10 11 12 13 14 15 16 17 18 19 20 21 **22** 23 24 25 26 27 28 29 30 31   MAY

Populations of the bittern, a wetland bird that was facing extinction in the UK in the late 1990s, have bounced back and are believed to be at a record high.

Resident numbers of 'Britain's loudest bird' have increased, where experts use its foghorn like booming call of the males to survey the species, counted an increase in the number of birds and including new sites.

RSPB Minsmere, where this shot was taken has always been a good location to spot this elusive bird, particularly early in the season before the reedbeds grow too high.

Bittern (Botaurus stellaris)   *840mm f6.3 1/320 ISO200*

Pied flycatcher (Ficedula hypoleuca)   *500mm f5 1/640 ISO1000*

Here is the beautiful pied flycatcher, photographed in woodlands in the south of Scotland. It's a summer visitor, breeding mainly in western areas, before returning to spend the winter in Western Africa.

1 2 3 4 5 6 7 8 9 10 11 12 13 14 15 16 17 18 19 20 21 22 23 24 25 26 27 28 29 30 31

Mute swan (Cygnus olor)   *500mm f8 1/1000 ISO1000*

One of the reasons for starting this project was that I wanted to get a shot of the cygnets riding on the parents' back soon after hatching. I've learnt a lot, for example that the cygnets don't leave the nest for the first 24 hours as they are not strong enough. This gives all of the eggs a chance to hatch before the mother takes them for their first swimming lesson and teaches them how to find food.

Mute swan (Cygnus olor)   *500mm f5 1/4000 ISO1250*

This shot captures the cuteness of the newly hatched cygnet, dependent on its mother for warmth and protection. It's only because of the trust I have built up with this pair that I was able to get close and share intimate moments like this.

'Catch of the day'. This kingfisher had caught the fish by stabbing it with its bill. In order to free it, he tossed his head back, throwing the fish into the air before catching it for a second time.

Kingfisher (Alcedo atthis)   *500mm f5 1/2000 ISO1600*

Little owl (Athene noctua)   *500mm f5.6 1/2500 ISO50*

A little owl emerges from a hole in a tree bordering a meadow full of buttercups. This gives the image background an unusual colour. Little owls breed in April/May when the adults are active during daylight hours, as well as at night.

The shot that everybody wants, a puffin with a beak full of sandeels. The characters of these birds are great and they really live up to their nick-name of sea parrot. This was taken on the Farne Islands off the coast of Northumberland.

The numbers of puffins here are said to have declined by 30% in the last 5 years for reasons not yet fully understood. Some suggest the warming of the North Sea is a significant factor.

Puffin (Fratercula arctica)　　　　*400mm f8 1/1250 ISO200*

MAY　1 2 3 4 5 6 7 8 9 10 11 12 13 14 15 16 17 18 19 20 21 22 23 24 25 26 27 28 29 30 31

Peregrine falcon (Falco peregrinus)

500mm f5 1/4000 ISO250

Some say they can fly at 240 mph when they dive, others say they can decapitate their prey on impact, and others that they can also hunt at night. We know for certain this is the fastest animal on the planet and one of the most spectacular and breathtaking hunters to watch. Their numbers are increasing as they utilise man made structures such as a cathedral spire for nesting.

1 2 3 4 5 6 7 8 9 10 11 12 13 14 15 16 17 18 19 20 21 22 23 24 25 26 27 28 29 30 31

MAY

Common buzzard (Buteo buteo)   *24mm f8 1/2000 ISO640*

This shot uses a wide angle lens and is as much about the beautiful scenery (of the Lake District) as it's about the subject. This is an example of where it can be beneficial to use captive birds to practice timing and creative techniques, producing something different to those wildlife shots taken from a hide with a long lens.

Puffin (Fratercula arctica)   *500mm f5 1/800 ISO400*

Puffins are a unique subject, as during the breeding season they demonstrate no fear of humans. I cannot think of many better ways to spend the day than sat beside a puffin colony watching them wander around you.

Common buzzard (Buteo buteo)   *600mm f6.3 1/2500 ISO800*

This is an example of blurring out the foreground and the background, leaving just the subject in focus. To achieve this you need a shallow depth of field but also the foreground and the background as far away from the subject as possible, in order for neither of these to be in focus.

JUN 1 2 3 4 5 6 7 8 9 10 11 12 13 14 15 16 17 18 19 20 21 22 23 24 25 26 27 28 29 30

Brown hare (Lepus europaeus)   *600mm f5.6 1/2500 ISO1000*

An example of a backlit subject. When you first start out with photography, you learn that the sun should be behind you thus lighting your subject. Every now and then it's worth breaking the rules by taking the shot directly into the sunlight, as this shot demonstrates.

According to some experts, in places where pine martens are on the increase, the number of grey squirrels is decreasing. One reason cited for this is that, compared to the reds, greys are less agile because they are heavier. As such, they spend much of their time on the ground and become easy prey for pine martens. Pine martens are therefore helping the red squirrels make a comeback in some areas of Scotland and Wales.

Pine marten (Martes martes)   *500mm f4 1/320 ISO4000*

Little owl (Athene noctua)   *210mm f8 1/200 ISO200*

As stated before, when photographing birds at the nest, great care needs to be taken so as not to scare the parents away and leave the young to perish. No image is worth harming the subject for.

Redstart (Phoenicurus phoenicurus)   *500mm f4 1/250 ISO1600*

The redstart was named for its red tail. Start comes from the old English steort, or "tail of an animal". This male is collecting insects for its young, located not very far away.

Little owl (Athene noctua)   *500mm f10 1/200 ISO100*

Believe it or not this shot was taken in the middle of a bright sunny day. The flash used in order to provide a black background picked out the subject and not the distant background. I love the stare from the owl in this shot.

Oystercatcher (Haematopus ostralegus)   *300mm f5.6 1/640 ISO400*

Easily identified by its large and bright orange bill, this bird was walking along a stone wall on the Shetland Islands where they can be photographed from the car. The bill is used to break into shellfish, with each individual inheriting a particular technique from its parents. Despite its name this wader does not usually eat oysters but favours mussels.

Little owl (Athene noctua)   *500mm f6.3 1/1600 ISO1000*

The little owl was introduced to Britain in the late 1880s to remove pests from rich landowners' gardens. It was then known as the 'fierce little foreigner'. As its Latin name implies, it was once associated with the Greek goddess Athene. Athene took the owl as her emblem which was printed on several Greek coins.

annet (Morus bassanus)

50mm f7.1 1/4000 ISO400

Scotland is home to around 60% of Europe's gannets. Bass rock has the world's largest colony of Northern gannets, with numbers peaking at over 150,000 from late January. Being surrounded by so many birds makes it very difficult to isolate a single subject.

1 2 3 4 5 6 7 8 9 10 11 12 13 14 15 16 17 18 19 20 21 22 23 24 25 26 27 28 29 30

Starling (Sturnus vulgaris) *600mm f5.6 1/1000 ISO1600*

Starlings look black from a distance but, when seen up close, they are glossy with a sheen of greens and purples. This bird was displaying on a post on the Shetland Islands where it could be approached by a vehicle without being disturbed, allowing it to enjoy the rest of its song.

ed deer (Cervus elaphus)   *47mm f4 1/320 ISO1000*

In early June the red deer young are born. They can be difficult to find as they are left hidden by their mums in thick vegetation, often in woodland. Be careful not to spend too long in one place, as even if you can't see the mum she will be nearby and keeping an eye on her young. Staying by the youngster will prevent her from returning and feeding it.

Red deer (Cervus elaphus)   *24mm f5.6 1/200 ISO2000*

If you go down to the woods today… You might come across a young deer. This red deer has been left by its mother because at this age, hiding is its best form of defence. The mother will return to feed the young at periodic intervals. Soon the youngster will be old enough to stay with its mum. As with all wildlife photography, you should always put the welfare of your subject first as no photograph is worth causing it unnecessary stress or harm. Only approach if it's absolutely safe to do so, and stay briefly to avoid causing disturbance or harm.

1 2 3 4 5 6 7 8 9 10 11 12 13 14 15 16 17 18 19 20 21 22 23 24 25 26 27 28 29 30

JUN

Fallow deer (Dama dama)   *40mm f5.6 1/500 ISO200*

A young fallow deer is typically born around the same time as the red deer but they tend to be found in open fields rather than woodland, which the red deer prefer. Again, the mum will leave her young to hide by remaining still, returning to feed it only when it's safe to do so.

Puffin (Fratercula arctica)   *300mm f5.6 1/2000 ISO800*

'Puffin in a sea of pink'. The puffin was laying in sea thrift on the cliffs of the Shetland Islands. Unlike the Farne Islands, as there are less visitors here, the cliffs are not roped off or fenced and hence their natural beauty is not spoiled.

1 2 3 4 5 6 7 8 9 10 11 12 13 14 15 16 17 18 19 20 21 22 23 24 25 26 27 28 29 30   JUN

Great skua (Stercorarius skua)   *600mm f5.6 1/1600 ISO1250*

'Great skua flypast'. As the females fly past, the male displays, stretching out his wings and calling. This species have increased in numbers on the Shetland Islands, slowly pushing the Arctic skuas out as they compete for nest sites. The great skua is also known locally as the bonxie.

Arctic tern (Sterna paradisaea)   *420mm f5.6 1/6400 ISO400*

The Arctic tern is well known for its long yearly migration. The journey from its Arctic breeding grounds to wintering habitats of Antarctica may cover 25,000 miles, and is the furthest yearly migration of any bird.

Shetland wren (Troglodytes troglodytes zetlandicus)   *420mm f5.6 1/2500 ISO1000*

Shetland Islands have always been a good place to photograph several species of birds. This is partly due to the large number of seabird colonies that breed on the cliffs surrounding the islands, but also partly due to having less predators than on the mainland, which makes them more approachable.

Fulmar (Fulmarus glacialis)   *420mm f7.1 1/5000 ISO800*

Coasts are often a good place to visit in order to practice your photography and in particular birds in flight. There are often strong uplifting breezes causing birds to appear almost motionless in the sky. This fulmar was doing exactly that and just hanging in the sky.

Wren (Troglodytes troglodytes)   *700mm f6.3 1/1250 ISO200*

Wrens are very territorial and often use the same perch to sing from, thus protecting their territory. This bird, photographed on Skomer Island, was in full song as I walked by. It didn't seem to notice me, or mind the camera as it continued with its song. I am always mindful not to cause any disturbance around birds' nests, thus keeping my visits and time spent as brief as possible.

Ringed plover (Charadrius hiaticula)   *420mm f7.1 1/3200 ISO800*

Ringed plovers have an amazing knack of just appearing on what you had previously thought was an empty beach. During the breeding season they will sometimes fake an injury and try to draw you away from their nest, or their young.

Puffin (Fratercula arctica)   *500mm f6.3 1/3200 ISO1600*

An unusual shot, as not many sites allow you to get close to puffins out at sea fishing. I would have loved to have got down even lower but the tide was coming in and already the breaking waves were soaking me.

Puffin (Fratercula arctica)   *500mm f4 1/8000 ISO400*

I am always amazed at the unique way in which puffins interact with humans. Perhaps it's because their colonies are visited by so many wishing to enjoy the spectacle they have become habituated whilst sitting on the cliff tops. In their environment, puffins are happy to come amongst people, as if we weren't there. Very few subjects allow you to get this close and it truly is an amazing experience.

1 2 3 4 5 6 7 8 9 10 11 12 13 14 15 16 17 18 19 20 21 22 **23** 24 25 26 27 28 29 30

JUN

Black guillemot (Cepphus grylle)   420mm f6.3 1/2000 ISO800

A stunning black and white bird. The legs and the inside of their mouths are a bright red, although only the legs can be seen in this image.

Purple heron (Ardea purpurea)
600mm f4 1/6400 ISO2500

The purple heron is a rare visitor to the UK, Isle of Man and Ireland with an average of 20 records per year. In 2010 this bird successfully bred in England for the first time. Chances of seeing a purple heron are at their highest during spring and autumn time as birds move between their breeding grounds and sub-Saharan Africa.

Puffins are a great subject and very entertaining to watch. However, it can be difficult to come up with a new (and different) image of such a well photographed species. For this shot, I wanted a silhouette of the puffin with the sunset behind it. With the majority of cliffs sloping downwards to the sea, it was difficult to get below the bird and have the sky behind it. So instead, I used the reflection of the colours in the sea.

Puffin (Fratercula arctica)   *500mm f6.3 1/1600 ISO800*

Puffin (Fratercula arctica)   *500mm f6.3 1/1600 ISO800*

Again something a little different. It's great to show a subject in its environment and capturing natural behaviour. This does exactly that, showing a puffin swimming underwater.

Common seal (Phoca vitulina)

500mm f4.5 1/500 ISO1000

Common seal pups, unlike those of grey seals, can swim almost immediately after birth. This allows common seals to breed on tidal sandbanks, while greys must pup above the high tide mark.

Common seal (Phoca vitulina)   *500mm f4 1/640 ISO800*

Also known as harbour seals, common seals are characteristic of sandflats and estuaries. The Wash of East Anglia is home to the UK's largest colony, although they are also found on rocky shores in Scotland. That was where I found this individual, early one morning when I was out looking for otters.

White-tailed eagle (Haliaeetus albicilla)   *371mm f8 1/2000 ISO1000*

White-tailed eagles are the UK's largest bird of prey. They became extinct in 1918 but changes in the legislation created an opportunity for their reintroduction. In 1975, 82 birds were transported from Norway to the Isle of Rum. More were released on the mainland and breeding has been successful with between 80-90 individual birds now living in Scotland. A five year plan has recently been announced to reintroduce these magnificent birds to the Isle of Wight and southern England too.

Oystercatcher (Haematopus ostralegus)   *500mm f4.5 1/5000 ISO400*

The oystercatcher nests on the beach, creating a small hollow in the shingle. If you walk along the beach during the summer months, you have to be really careful not to tread on their eggs as they are so well camouflaged.

Barn owl (Tyto alba) *500mm f5 1/1600 ISO500*

Sometimes a car can be used as a hide if you are fortunate enough to find wildlife close to the road. Often birds such as barn owls or kestrels do not associate vehicles with danger, much to their cost as so many of them are killed beside the roads where they hunt. However, as soon as you attempt to get out of the car they will recognise the human form and disappear.

Avocet (Recurvirostra avosetta) 700mm f8 1/1000 ISO50

This is another of the UK's best recognised birds, particularly as it has been the symbol for the RSPB from around 1955. The reason this bird was chosen is due to the avocet being one of the UK's most successful reintroductions of a species which had previously been wiped out. Now 50% of the population in the UK can be found in RSPB reserves. Despite its success story, this bird is still a schedule 1 protected species and requires a licence to photograph it at or near the nest.

1 2 3 4 5 6 7 8 9 10 11 12 13 14 15 16 17 18 19 20 21 22 23 24 25 26 27 28 29 30 31 JUL

Otter (Lutra lutra)   *75mm f5.6 1/250 ISO1000*

An environmental shot of a pond and two of its nocturnal visitors. It's always great to observe behaviour and the 'pecking order' in the natural world. As shown here with the grey heron watching from a safe distance.

Kestrel (Falco tinnunculus)   *500mm f5 1/1600 ISO500*

This is a young kestrel, identifiable by its markings and the few downy feathers remaining on its head. The chicks fledge at 27–32 days old but they are still reliant on their parents for food. They become fully independent at 7–8 weeks old and they reach sexual maturity at 1 year old, although as with many birds of prey, they do not usually mate during their first year of maturity.

Pine marten (Martes martes)   *312mm f5.6 1/500 ISO1250*

Pine martens are the only mustelids with semi-retractable claws. This enables them to lead more arboreal lifestyles, such as climbing or running on trees and branches where they often hunt their prey. They are omnivores with a varied diet.

Highland cow (Bos taurus) *500mm f5.6 1/500 ISO64*

Not truly wildlife, however Highland cattle are an iconic species of the Highlands of Scotland and are very photogenic subjects. This cow was photographed roaming free on the Isle of Mull.

Great crested grebe (Podiceps cristatus)   *700mm f5.6 1/1600 ISO800*

An adult great crested grebe turning the eggs on its floating nest. The adults share the incubation of the eggs, switching at regular intervals to allow the other to feed. This photo was taken using a floating hide from a distance so as not to disturb the nesting birds.

Turtle dove (Streptopelia turtur)   *500mm f4 1/1600 ISO400*

'Turtle dove calling'. Somebody once told me the key to becoming a good wildlife photographer was to capture images that will be interesting to others. If the only description of a photograph is the subject's name then it's not going to appeal to many. A solution is to ensure the subject is always doing something. I'll let you make up your own mind. This turtle dove is calling to its mate.

A handsome shot of a hare looking straight down the lens of the camera. With some subjects it's all about fieldcraft, making yourself invisible, being still and quiet, and letting the wildlife come to you.

I always try to leave the wildlife as I find it, which means not disturbing it or scaring it away. Even if I am in a hide, I don't leave it with the subject in view, as I never want the wildlife to associate the hide with humans.

Brown hare (Lepus europaeus)   *600mm f4 1/5000 ISO2500*

1 2 3 4 5 6 7 8 9 10 11 12 13 14 15 16 17 18 19 20 21 22 23 24 25 26 27 28 29 30 31

JUL

Puffin (Fratercula arctica)   *600mm f8 1/4000 ISO1000*

As always with wildlife, it's expect the unexpected. Previously just floating around on the sea, then, all of a sudden it's running across the surface to get airborne. The secret to achieving shots like this, is to be set up ready for the action. Slow shutter speeds are fine for stationary subjects, but often there is no warning before something bursts into action.

Sparrowhawk (Accipiter nisus)

500mm f4 1/1000 ISO2500

The beautiful male sparrowhawk is an extremely fast bird. Whilst this can have its disadvantages when trying to capture it in flight, it can also provide an opportunity. Here a slow shutter speed was used to capture the movement of the wings.

Gannet (Morus bassanus) *182mm f6.3 1/2500 ISO1600*

Gannets are Britain's largest seabird and have a very distinctive plumage. However, the young are brown and with each passing season they become progressively whiter, reaching the complete adult plumage in their fourth or fifth year.

The tawny owl is the familiar 'brown owl' of the UK's woodlands, parks and gardens. Listen out for the famous 'twit-twoo' call, actually made up of a 'ke-wick' sound from a female and an answering 'hoo-hoo-ooo' from a male. Or in other words, it's the female making the 'twit' call and the male the 'twoo'.

Tawny owl (Strix aluco)   *600mm f5.6 1/2000 ISO1600*

Puffin (Fratercula arctica)   *400mm f7.1 1/4000 ISO2500*

An incoming puffin on Skomer Island. This picture is taken against the sun light, enabling the sun to show through the wing feathers and making the background dark to help the subject stand out.

Roe deer (Capreolus capreolus)

500mm f4 1/800 ISO2000

Roe deer are a common variety of our native deer, favouring farmland and woodland. July is the main breeding season for roe deer, when the males rut to defend their territory and win the right to mate with the females. However the female's fertilised egg does not implant until mid-winter, meaning the young will not be born until the next spring.

JUL 1 2 3 4 5 6 7 8 9 10 11 12 13 14 15 16 17 18 19 20 21 22 23 24 25 26 27 28 29 30 31

Barn owl (Tyto alba)   *500mm f4 1/800 ISO100*

Another example of blurring the foreground and the background, making the subject stand out. In this case a barn owl hunting the edges of cropped fields.

Kingfisher (Alcedo atthis)   *55mm f18 1/200 ISO1000*

An extremely rare opportunity to see inside the nesting chamber of a kingfisher. This image was shot under a special licence with the licence holder present. We only had five minutes to set up and take the photo in order to keep disturbance to a minimum.

Brimstone (Gonepteryx rhamni)   *400mm f14 1/1600 ISO800*

This image of a brimstone butterfly shows a macro lens isn't always required to obtain an image of our smaller wildlife.

Osprey (Pandion haliaetus)   *278mm f5 1/3200 ISO1600*

Osprey arrive back in the UK in April and they are quick to pair up, with the female soon laying and incubating their eggs. During this time, it's only the males that fish, and often a dominant male will try to hold a good fishing spot and prevent other males from fishing. Once the young are old enough to be left on the nest alone, the females once again start fishing. July sees the fledglings also learning how to fish in order to survive before their great migration.

JUL   1 2 3 4 5 6 7 8 9 10 11 12 13 14 15 16 17 18 19 20 21 22 23 24 25 26 27 28 29 30 31

Great crested grebe (Podiceps cristatus)   *600mm f9 1/1600 ISO640*

Great crested grebes teach their young to swim by carrying them on their back (as above) and then diving, leaving the chicks on the surface. They emerge a few feet away so that the chicks can swim back onto them.

Deer such as this female fallow deer (doe) and its young fawn can often be photographed in deer parks, such as the Royal Parks; Bushy and Richmond in London.

Fallow deer (Dama dama)　　　*600mm f4 1/640 ISO200*

Barn owl (Tyto alba)   *14mm f5.6 1/200 ISO250*

This image was taken using a wide angle lens, capturing the subject and its environment just as the sun was setting.

Swallows undertake an impressive 6,000 mile migration between the UK and South Africa twice a year.

They nest in the UK in the summer, but as they only feed on aerial insects, their food source starts to run out in the autumn.

Obtaining flight shots such as this can often be achieved by pre focusing on a point where you expect the subject to be. This swallow was coming in to land, and therefore it was possible to focus on the branch to achieve this shot.

Swallow (Hirundo rustica)   *600mm f5.6 1/500 ISO250*

Great spotted woodpecker (Dendrocopos major)   *600mm f5 1/3200 ISO2500*

The 'drumming' of a great spotted woodpecker is a familiar sound of our woodlands, parks and gardens. It's a form of communication and is mostly used to mark territories and to display in spring.

Common redshanks are often the first of the waders to panic and give noisy alarm calls as they depart. However, this shot was taken on the Shetland Islands where they are less wary and can often be seen on posts beside the road and photographed from the car.

Redshank (Tringa totanus)   *600mm f5.6 1/2000 ISO1600*

JUL   1 2 3 4 5 6 7 8 9 10 11 12 13 14 15 16 17 18 19 20 21 22 23 24 25 26 27 28 29 30 31

Grey heron (Ardea cinerea)   *182mm f5.6 1/250 ISO1600*

Photography is often about 'the moment'. Here I wanted to capture the heron fishing, with the beak under the surface, but the eye still visible. In this image the reflection and the lilies were an added bonus.

1 2 3 4 5 6 7 8 9 10 11 12 13 14 15 16 17 18 19 20 21 22 23 24 25 26 27 28 29 30 31   JUL

Photography is a form of art and, as with all art, people have different tastes. Not to everyone's liking, this image focuses on the reflection in the dewdrop, rather than on the subject itself.

Seven spot ladybird (Coccinella septempunctata)   *37mm f22 1/250 ISO100*

Harvest mouse (Micromys minutus) *100mm f14 1/160 ISO200*

Harvest mice eat a mixture of seeds, berries and insects, and as in this case they sometimes take grain from cereal heads. This image was not taken using a macro lens, but a telephoto lens instead. When using a telephoto lens to photograph subjects relatively close up, you will need to increase the depth of field.

This is a buzzard that I'd rescued. It was sat on a field and refused to fly. Normally I would leave it alone and not interfere but I knew the farmer would be walking his dogs shortly and, all being off their leads, they would have made short work of him. I took him into a RSPCA centre, thinking it was a young bird that had flown the nest too early. However, they could tell by the faded wing feathers that this was not a young bird. They looked after him for several weeks until he began to fly again, and shortly afterwards, I was able to release him back to where I had found him.

Common buzzard (Buteo buteo)   *500mm f4 1/320 ISO800*

Gannet (Morus bassanus)   *180mm f6.3 1/6400 ISO1600*

Spending time watching gannets dive is an incredible experience, but as with all photography, knowing your subject is an advantage. Before it dives, the gannet calls out. This is not to warn other birds beneath it, but it's thought the gannet is simply taking in air before it dives.

Osprey (Pandion haliaetus)　　　　　　　　　　　　　　　　　　*500mm f4.5 1/2500 ISO3200*

There are approximately 200 pairs of nesting ospreys in Scotland, taking up almost every available nest site. This is an amazing sight, an osprey circling in the sky above the loch, calling, before suddenly dropping out of the sky and snatching a fish from just under the surface. Some birds, like this one, come in like a rocket, hitting the water at such speed that it becomes submerged, except for the head. It then takes a few beats of its large wings to become airborne, especially when carrying a large fish.

Osprey (Pandion haliatus)   *500mm f4 1/1600 ISO5000*

Ospreys visit the UK from April to breed, before returning to Africa in August. Usually the females and the young leave first, they're later followed by the males at the end of August. The osprey turn the fish they catch with their feet in order to carry it like a torpedo and make it more streamlined.

Kingfisher (Alcedo atthis)   *255mm f7.1 1/5000 ISO4000*

A kingfisher diving; this shot requires an exceptionally fast shutter speed of at least 1/5000 of a second to freeze the dive as it's so fast. Good light and an exceptionally high ISO are also required in order to achieve this.

Rabbit (Oryctolagus cuniculus)　　　　　　　　　　　　　*600mm f5 1/2500 ISO500*

Baby rabbits are often a great photography subject as they have not yet learnt to fear humans. When laying still and quiet outside a warren, it may not be long before the youngsters come out to feed and play.

Green woodpeckers are the largest of the three species of woodpecker we have in the UK, and also the one which spends the least amount of time in the trees. They also like to excavate their own nest holes, a process that can take them from two to four weeks.

Green woodpecker (Picus viridis)   *600mm f4 1/100 ISO800*

Kingfisher (Alcedo atthis)   *255mm f7.1 1/2000 ISO2500*

This is a shot of the kingfisher doing what the kingfisher does best, diving under water in order to catch a fish.

Common buzzard (Buteo buteo)

40mm f8 1/2500 ISO800

The common buzzard loves to drift on thermals generated by hills and valleys. This image shows the broad wings used for soaring and explains how often people mistake this bird for a golden eagle in Scotland.

Gannet (Morus bassanus)   *175mm f6.3 1/4000 ISO1600*

Gannets are famous for their ability to dive into the sea at speeds of up to 60 mph and swim underwater. They have streamlined bodies adapted for plunge-diving at high speed, including powerful neck muscles, and a spongy bone plate at the base of the bill. The nostrils are inside the bill and can be closed to prevent water entry and the eyes are protected by strong nictitating membranes.

Grass snake (Natrix natrix)

400mm f8 1/800 ISO3200

Grass snakes prey predominately on amphibians and hence can often be found around water, including garden ponds. Another way of attracting these reptiles to your garden is to have a compost heap, as this is where they like to lay their eggs.

Mallard (Anas platyrhynchos)   *500mm f4.5 1/500 ISO1000*

This is an image of a common subject doing a routine task such as drinking. However, the low angle and the greens of the background help make the image work.

On moorlands, meadow pipits are the most common 'foster parents' of young cuckoos. The adult cuckoo will lay a single egg in a meadow pipit's nest. After hatching, the cuckoo chick will push the other eggs or young birds out of the nest, giving its foster parents more time to concentrate on feeding the intruder.

Meadow pipit (Anthus pratensis)   *600mm f6.3 1/800 ISO500*

White-tailed eagle (Haliaeetus albicilla)   *400mm f8 1/2000 ISO1250*

At the time of writing, plans have just been announced to reintroduce the UK's largest bird of prey to the south coast of England. White-tailed eagles with a wingspan of up to 2.5m (8ft) were once widespread but were wiped out in the UK a century ago. Plans for a five-year reintroduction programme based on the Isle of Wight have just been given the go ahead.

Osprey (Pandion haliaetus)   *400mm f8 1/800 ISO3200*

An image I'd wanted to achieve for a while and just in time before the birds return to Africa for the winter. It's often a good idea to approach a subject with an image you wish to achieve already in mind. Sometimes you will have to sacrifice other images in pursuit of achieving that goal.

Avocet (Recurvirostra avosetta)   *700mm f11 1/800 ISO500*

All birds are protected, but some species, like these avocets, have additional protection during the breeding season, as do their nests, eggs and dependent young. This image was taken under licence issued by Natural England. Further information can be found on the relevant websites.

The point of contact. Action shots are often all about the 'timing'. The digital age and speed of cameras, allows multiple images to be taken in a quick burst. When considering action shots you should have your camera set up for high speed bursts and not be afraid to 'machine gun' providing the subject allows it. You will end up with a lot of images to review and maybe delete, but hopefully also with that perfect shot you were after such as this, with the kingfisher touching the surface of the water.

Kingfisher (Alcedo atthis)   *176mm f8 1/5000 ISO4000*

Kingfisher (Alcedo atthis)   *500mm f8 1/500 ISO100*

This image is all about determination. It's not news to many people that during the breeding season a male kingfisher will catch a fish and offer it to his mate, cementing their bond. This is an image I have wanted to capture for years, the fish pass. I have observed it a number of times, but usually from a distance or hidden in vegetation. I had witnessed this fish pass the previous weekend, but was unable to capture it, so I kept returning early every morning, until finally over a week later, I got a second chance.

Barn owl (Tyto alba)   *95mm f5.6 1/250 ISO400*

A barn owl sitting in a window of an old farm building. The light is fading, however this bird is out before dusk, meaning it's probably feeding young or the weather conditions were not ideal for hunting during the previous night.

AUG 1 2 3 4 5 6 7 8 9 10 11 12 13 14 15 16 17 18 19 20 21 22 23 24 25 26 27 28 29 30 31

Common buzzard (Buteo buteo)   *300mm f5.6 1/320 ISO200*

Buzzards are one of the laziest hunters in the bird of prey world and the most common in the UK. Often they will sit on posts and wait for their prey to come to them. They also eat road kill to save them from having to hunt at all.

Raven (Corvus corax)   *600mm f5.6 1/2500 ISO800*

Another example of how getting low down and, in this example, blurring both the foreground and the background can make the subject stand out.

Gannet (Morus bassanus) and herring gull (Larus argentatus)   *170mm f8 1/3200 ISO640*

An image showing different species competing for the same food. In this instance, I'm not sure whether the herring gull wants to eat the fish, the gannet or both.

Osprey (Pandion haliaetus)

500mm f4.5 1/1600 ISO400

A bird which I have travelled many times to Scotland to see and photograph, but usually when diving at speed into the water. This location provided an opportunity to see the osprey up close and relatively still. It has enforced the size and power of their wings, which they use to get themselves airborne when submerged in the water.

Osprey (Pandion haliaetus) 500mm f4 1/500 ISO200

Many birds fluff their feathers up, or 'rouse' before they take off. This is their way of clearing their feathers of debris, kind of like a pre-flight check.

Again an example of getting low down and at eye level with the subject, in this case a fox. Laying in mud or nettles, like I was to obtain this shot, can be uncomfortable but the results can make it worthwhile.

Red fox (Vulpes vulpes)   *114mm f5 1/6400 ISO500*

Water vole (Arvicola amphibius)   *400mm f5.6 1/1000 ISO 1250*

Scottish water voles have a completely different ancestry to their southern cousins across the border. Voles migrated to England from south east Europe, recolonising after the Ice Age. Scottish voles came from the Iberian Peninsula.

Barn owl (Tyto alba)   *170mm f8 1/200 ISO1600*

A magical moment when the young barn owls commenced the fledging process. There were four young at this site and they began leaving the barn, encouraged by the adults to explore the big wide world. It was an amazing sight to watch them as they flew around the farmyard, making brief flights and calling out to the adults. This image was shot under licence with the licence holder present.

Red grouse (Lagopus lagopus scoticus) 500mm f5 1/800 ISO400

'Red grouse and a fly'. Red grouse can be found in the Highlands of Scotland. However during the shooting season, which opens in August, they may become less approachable. They can also be found in Yorkshire and other areas. Males can be photographed well from February through to May as they are very territorial. In August the heather turns pink, offering a different kind of photographic opportunity.

Little grebe (Tachybaptus ruficollis)   *500mm f4 1/400 ISO400*

The smallest of the grebe family. It often dives when disturbed, resurfacing some distance away. This image is all about the soft pastel colours reflected in the water. This book often shows consecutive days with the same subject. This is because sometimes the first trip is a fact finding mission, and I don't expect to gain much photographically. I then revisit the following day with the benefit of what I'd learnt from the previous visit.

AUG   1 2 3 4 5 6 7 8 9 10 11 12 13 14 15 16 17 18 19 20 21 22 23 24 25 26 **27** 28 29 30 31

Little grebe (Tachybaptus ruficollis) 500mm f4 1/400 ISO800

Here is a family shot as one of the adults continues to brood the young and any unhatched eggs on the nest, while the other collects food to bring back for the young. To achieve this image I had to build a hide in the water, using a tree for support. I knelt in my waders to achieve a water level shot; but unfortunately it cost me my mobile phone.

An almost perfect reflection. In water which is neither tidal nor flowing and on calm days, great reflections are possible. This image has the sun on the subject which adds to the strength of the reflection.

Black-tailed godwit (Limosa limosa)   600mm f5.6 1/400 ISO200

AUG   1 2 3 4 5 6 7 8 9 10 11 12 13 14 15 16 17 18 19 20 21 22 23 24 25 26 27 28 **29** 30 31

Grey heron (Ardea cinerea)   *500mm f6.3 1/640 ISO1000*

In certain parks and other public places grey herons have become used to people and therefore don't mind a close up. This one at Richmond Park almost looks as if it's posing for a selfie.

Hedgehog (Erinaceus europaeus) *600mm f4 1/500 ISO800*

As many know, the hedgehog is covered in short spines for defence and, in addition, they can roll up into a ball. Surveys show they have between 5,000–7,000 spines. Each spine lasts about a year then drops out and a replacement is grown.

Skylark (Alauda arvensis)

600mm f8 1/4000 ISO2500

Skylark chicks are extremely well hidden. They even have long hairs on the top of their heads to aid their camouflage by blending in with the grasses.

Gannet (Morus bassanus)   *170mm f8 1/3200 ISO800*

Gannets by name and certainly gannets by nature. Here, the three birds are squabbling over the same fish. Often a bird will attempt to swallow the whole fish, as it surfaces, to avoid sharing or losing it completely. This time the fish broke into three parts and they all got a piece.

Gannet (Morus bassanus)

110mm f8 1/3200 ISO500

A shot of the gannet as it's about to break the surface and the remaining water runs down its head. This bird is lucky; as it hasn't yet been spotted, it may get to enjoy the fish by itself.

Barn owl (Tyto alba)   *24mm f7.1 1/250 ISO1600*

A continuation of the barn owl project. Despite working with this bird for almost three years now, I never see her during daylight hours. This is the closest I have got, just as the sun had set. A little fill-in flash was used to light the bird, otherwise it would have been a silhouette against the lighter sky.

Barn owl (Tyto alba)   *24mm f5.6 1/5 ISO 2000*

A similar shot to the previous one, but on the following night. Just changing the angle and the distance to the subject can make a huge difference.

Kestrel (Falco tinnunculus)   *500mm f4 1/1600 ISO400*

A young kestrel sitting pretty in pink heather. Kestrels prefer open habitats, such as heathland, fields, shrubland or marshes. They can often be spotted hovering in the sky, or sitting perched on high vantage points, such as electricity wires, and watching the ground beneath them.

Golden eagle (Aquila chrysaetos)   *182mm f5 1/2000 ISO4000*

Golden eagles stay in upland areas all year round but can be more visible in late summer and autumn when the young fledge and take to the wing. Hotspots for eagles can be found along the west coast and the islands from Mull and Lochaber, north and west through Skye to Lewis.

Flash lighting can allow more creativity. This wild owl was lit from both sides and slightly behind to allow the light to shine through the feathers and particularly the wings.

It presents a different image, but may not be to everyone's taste. Photography at the end of the day is a form of art, and as such is subjective.

Tawny owl (Strix aluco)   *300mm f8 1/125 ISO1600*

Barn owl (Tyto alba)

286mm f5.6 1/5000 ISO2000

Always a magical sight, watching the silent flight of a barn owl hunting low over undisturbed grassland. A barn owl hunts by sound rather than sight. With its acute hearing it can detect the slightest movement or sound of its prey. The ears are set asymmetrically, meaning one ear is higher than the other. They are located under the feathering of the inside edge of the facial disc, next to the eyes. The facial disc acts as an amazing sound funnel, collecting and filtering sound. This allows the owl to pinpoint its prey with complete accuracy.

1 2 3 4 5 6 7 8 9 10 11 12 13 14 15 16 17 18 19 20 21 22 23 24 25 26 27 28 29 30

SEP

Common seal (Phoca vitulina)   *500mm f4.5 1/800 ISO1000*

This baby common seal is already at home in the water. They can swim from only a few hours old, which differs greatly from the grey seal pups that rarely swim for the first three weeks, until they have moulted their soft white baby fur.

Little owl (Athene noctua)   *500mm f5.6 1/1250 ISO80*

It's believed that Florence Nightingale rescued an owl chick that had fallen from its nest in Athens, Greece. She named the owl "Athena". This owl then became her devoted companion. The owl would perch on her finger for feeding and often travelled with her in her pocket. It died in 1855 and its preserved remains are now on display in the Florence Nightingale museum in London.

Dolphin (Tursiops truncatus)   *400mm f8 1/2000 ISO1000*

One of the best places to see and photograph dolphins from the land is Chanonry Point on the east coast of Scotland. Dolphin activity here is influenced by the tide. The best time to see them is in the summer months and on a rising tide when they start to chase the fish against the sandbanks. I have often sat on the beach beside the lighthouse from low tide waiting for these amazing creatures to show and put on a performance.

Stonechat (Saxicola torquata)   *600mm f4 1/2500 ISO3200*

Common gorse or the closely related western gorse can bloom at almost any time of the year. This makes it very attractive to insects and therefore birds. In addition, the evergreen thorny branches make it a safe haven for spiders during some of the harshest winters. This means it can often be very profitable to set your camera up around this kind of habitat and wait to see what turns up, in this case a male stonechat.

Cuteness overload! A harvest mouse as it has decided to have a quick wash. These adorable mammals are great subjects, always busy and on the move. It's surprising just how much depth of field is required for such a tiny subject, in order to get it sharp where it matters.

Harvest mouse (Micromys minutus)400mm f6.3 1/1250 ISO1600

Red fox (Vulpes vulpes)   *148mm f5.6 1/2500 ISO400*

Red foxes live around the world in many diverse habitats including forests, grasslands, mountains, and deserts. They also adapt well to human environments such as farms, suburban areas, and even larger cities. The red fox's resourcefulness has earned it a legendary reputation for intelligence and cunning.

Kingfisher (Alcedo atthis)   *85mm f8 1/2500 ISO4000*

Many kingfisher images are taken in commercial hides and using diving tables etc. I wanted to show this kingfisher in its environment and therefore used a wide angled lens to photograph it diving in this pond amongst the lilies and the water weed.

Kingfisher (Alcedo atthis)   *500mm f8 1/5000 ISO800*

This is the same set up as the previous shot, but this time using a 500mm lens to zoom in on the bird. It's amazing how the same set up can result in such different images.

Hawfinch (Coccothraustes coccothraustes)   *500mm f8 1/320 ISO2000*

A lovely bird and one that I had always wanted to photograph, a hawfinch. I was lucky enough to spend time in a hide with a drinking pool and often a single bird would come to drink or bathe. This image shows a pair, the male on the left and the female on the right, and both in focus. I have since built my own drinking pool in my back garden and the number of species that will visit a source of water, especially during dry spells when alternatives are limited is incredible.

Jay (Garrulus glandarius)   *500mm f5.6 1/1000 ISO1600*

Bad hair jay! Another example of a visitor that welcomes a vital source of water during a spell of warm weather. On days when the temperature rose above 20 degrees Celsius the number of visitors to the pool doubled.

Kingfisher (Alcedo atthis)

500mm f10 1/1250 ISO800

The more you watch a subject, the more you can learn about it. This is not a territorial dispute as this is actually a breeding pair of kingfishers. It seems they still have disagreements, just like a married couple.

Avocet (Recurvirostra avosetta)   *400mm f6.3 1/1600 ISO200*

The avocet is a distinctively patterned black and white wader with a long up-curved beak. This bird is the emblem of the RSPB and symbolises the bird protection movement in the UK. Its return in the 1940s and the subsequent increase in numbers represents one of the most successful conservation and protection projects, hence why it was chosen as their emblem.

Blue tits time the hatching of their young for spring, when there should be a plentiful supply of caterpillars to feed them. However during autumn they switch to include seeds and fruit into their diet.

Blue tit (Cyanistes caeruleus)   *370mm f16 1/250 ISO320*

Common frog (Rana temporaria)   *300mm f13 1/400 ISO160(*

Outside the breeding season common frogs live a solitary life in damp places. They are active for much of the year, only hibernating in the coldest months. In the most extreme conditions they may be trapped under ice for a period of time, where the oxygen intake through their skin suffices to sustain the needs of the cold and motionless frogs during this period of hibernation.

Fly agaric is probably our most recognisable species of fungus, with the mushroom's now distinctive red cap and white stalk. Fly agaric is found in woodlands, parks and heaths with scattered trees, typically growing beneath birch trees or pines and spruces. The colourful fungus is known to be toxic and therefore rarely eaten, but can provide a welcome perch.

Great tit (Parus major)   *600mm f5.6 1/4000 ISO2500*

SEP 1 2 3 4 5 6 7 8 9 10 11 12 13 14 15 16 17 18 19 20 21 22 23 24 25 26 27 28 29 30

Fallow deer (Dama dama)   *500mm f4.5 1/1000 ISO2000*

For some reason I am a real fan of just one eye showing in my subject. It appears to focus the attention more and shows a connection with the subject through the lens.

Chinese water deer (Hydropotes inermis)   *600mm f5.6 1/5000 ISO1600*

It will come as no surprise that this deer originated from China (and Korea). The numbers in the UK have grown and now account for 10% of the world's population. Instead of the usual antlers that other deer in the UK have, male Chinese water deer have long canine teeth that measure up to 8 cm long and look like fangs.

Polecat (Mustela putorius)   *349mm f5.6 1/1600 ISO250*

It's unclear whether polecats are native to the UK or not. They are one of only three British mammals not to have a Celtic-derived Welsh name; the other two being fallow deer and rabbit which we know were both introduced.

The peregrine falcon hunts and captures its prey in mid-air. It strikes the prey with a clenched foot, usually in one wing so it does not injure itself, stunning or killing it with the impact. If the prey is too heavy to carry, the peregrine will drop it to the ground and eat it there.

Peregrine falcon (Falco peregrinus)   *300mm f5.6 1/500 ISO400*

Otter (Lutra lutra)   *371mm f5.6 1/4000 ISO400*

Otters are becoming more common and sometimes in certain areas individuals will become regular visitors, even during daylight hours. This, like a rare bird, can attract the crowds and sometimes idiotic behaviour. I know of one such site where photographers would take tins of sardines to entice the otters. Not exactly their usual food; where would they find a tin opener?

1 2 3 4 5 6 7 8 9 10 11 12 13 14 15 16 17 18 19 20 21 22 23 24 25 26 27 28 29 30

SEP

The aim of this image was to get low down in order to throw the foreground, as well as the background out of focus. As this was bracken its colour nicely matched the bird, but it's a technique that makes the bird stand out.

Common buzzard (Buteo buteo)   *500mm f4 1/800 ISO250*

Golden eagle (Aquila chrysaetos)   *500mm f4 1/320 ISO20*

A similar example to the previous image, a low vantage point making the subject in this case a beautiful golden eagle stand out from the long grass.

Kestrels need to eat between 4 and 8 voles a day, depending on the time of the year and the amount of energy-consuming hover-hunting they do. They may catch several voles in quick succession, caching some for later.

The stored food is usually eaten the same day just before dusk. This reduces the risk of going to roost on an empty stomach.

Kestrel (Falco tinnunculus)   *500mm f5 1/1250 ISO800*

Red kite (Milvus milvus)   *600mm f4 1/1600 ISO200*

Kites usually hunt on the wing, soaring and circling over open ground. They are mainly carrion eaters, but are quite capable of killing small mammals and birds. Road-casualty pheasants, rabbits and squirrels form an important part of the diet of the reintroduced kites in England.

Red deer (Cervus elaphus)   *500mm f4 1/1000 ISO1000*

Late September is the start of the red deer rut, with the peak being in the first couple of weeks of October. Many wildlife enthusiasts descend upon the Royal Parks of London where numbers of these magnificent beasts and the likelihood of being able to witness their spectacle are great. The fact they are used to people makes them easier to be observed.

Red deer (Cervus elaphus)   *500mm f4 1/1000 ISO2000*

Taken on a wet day, this stag roared amongst the bracken. The subdued light brought the colours together and, despite getting soaked, made for a very successful day. It just shows that sometimes great pictures can be produced in the worst weather conditions. It's worth reminding ourselves that a winning photo has never been taken with the camera staying dry, or the photographer for that matter!

Red deer (Cervus elaphus)   *500mm f4 1/1000 ISO1600*

I make no apologies for using several images of the same species this month, as the red deer is the largest land mammal in the UK, and their rut is one of the greatest spectacles to witness. Two heavyweights go head to head in this image, neither backing down until exhaustion finally defeats them both.

Red deer (Cervus elaphus)   *500mm f4.5 1/1250 ISO1000*

A simple image of a red deer drinking from a puddle. This stag was thirsty after so much roaring. It was nice to show some calm during the chaos of the rut.

Red deer (Cervus elaphus)   *400mm f10 1/30 ISO100*

Slow panning a subject has the effect of blurring the background and the movement of the legs, whilst keeping the eye sharp. Shutter speeds vary, depending on the movement of the subject, but 1/20th of a second is a good starting place.

Red deer (Cervus elaphus)

500mm f5 1/1250 ISO1250

Envisioning an image in black and white is a useful skill to have. The light dried grass contrasts well with the dark textured fur of this stag. I knew I was going to convert this image before I had even pressed the shutter.

Red deer (Cervus elaphus)

400mm f5 1/8000 ISO4000

Early morning can be the best time to photograph wildlife, as there are less people around, and the light is at its best. This backlit shot of a deer in the early morning light is another example of shooting against the sun.

OCT 1 2 3 4 5 6 7 8 9 10 11 12 13 14 15 16 17 18 19 20 21 22 23 24 25 26 27 28 29 30 31

Tawny owl (Strix aluco)   *500mm f5.6 1/1000 ISO400*

Photographers are often looking for props to add to their images, and in the autumn, fungi can add some useful colour to an image.

As already stated reflections are a favourite of mine. This time a fallow deer came to a lake in the woods to drink. During hot days, and if water in the area is limited, it can often pay to stakeout a waterhole as several species will come to drink at various times during the day.

Fallow deer (Dama dama)   *349mm f8 1/2500 ISO640*

Robin (Erithacus rubecula)   *600mm f5.6 1/2500 ISO2500*

The European robin is one of Britain's best known birds, which is probably why it was declared Britain's national bird.

1 2 3 4 5 6 7 8 9 10 11 12 **13** 14 15 16 17 18 19 20 21 22 23 24 25 26 27 28 29 30 31

OCT

Fallow deer (Dama dama)   *370mm f5.6 1/2000 ISO500*

As October unfolds, it's the fallow deer that take centre stage and begin their rut, shortly after the red deer. Early one morning I spotted these three bucks sizing each other up. I call this image, 'Three Kings'. Originally, the deer on the right was behind the one in the centre. I had to wait for it to move in order to get the shot, otherwise it looked like a deer with two heads. They say good things come to those who wait...

Fallow deer (Dama dama)   *160mm f5.6 1/320 ISO250*

The early morning light at sunrise, the golden hour. Intensified by a misty and frosty morning following a clear, cold night, the light was magical. This lone buck stood under a tree framing it in the first rays of light.

Kingfisher (Alcedo atthis)　　　　　　　　　　*500mm f4.5 1/500 ISO800*

The male kingfisher can be distinguished from the female easily by the colour of its lower bill. The male has a black bill whereas the female's is reddy-orange, or a 'lipstick'.

Kingfisher (Alcedo atthis)   *500mm f5 1/250 ISO100*

A similar image to the previous page, but this time using fill-in flash which has the effect of darkening the background. If you have a subject visiting a location often, it's good to try and 'mix up' your set up in order to obtain a variety of images.

A lovely male bearded tit picking at the seed heads of a reedbed. Remarkably, these birds switch their diet from insects in the summer months to seeds during the winter.

There are estimated to be less than 500 pairs in the UK, making them one of the UK's rarest birds. They are mainly found on the east and southern coast areas but also in north Wales, restricted to reedbed areas such as Minsmere in Suffolk.

Bearded tit (Panurus biarmicus)   *400mm f5.6 1/1000 ISO800*

OCT 1 2 3 4 5 6 7 8 9 10 11 12 13 14 15 16 17 18 19 20 21 22 23 24 25 26 27 28 29 30 31

Red deer (Cervus elaphus) *500mm f5 1/500 ISO1000*

Before any fighting, the challenge from another stag commences vocally. If this isn't enough, the rivals parallel walk to size each other up. And if neither backs down the locking of antlers finally decides the contest.

Wigeon (Anas penelope) *500mm f4.5 1/250 ISO800*

Wigeon, also known as the whistling duck. Late October to early November sees the numbers of many duck species swell dramatically. Migrants flock to the UK's wetlands to escape harsher winters elsewhere. The visitors include over 400,000 wigeon. The drake pictured above is one of our smartest ducks, yet the first thing that often draws your attention to this bird is its high-pitched whistle, once described as the sound a child makes when going down a slide.

Tufted duck (Aythya fuligula)   *500mm f5 1/200 ISO250*

This shot shows how sometimes it's all about the background. A shot of a female tufted duck by itself wouldn't be that interesting. However here it's complemented by the colour reflected in the water from the vegetation around the lake.

Barn owls usually nest in spring, however they have been recorded as breeding in every month of the year in the UK. As the young fledge, the adults will often hunt further afield in order to allow the young to hunt close to the nest site.

Barn owl (Tyto alba)   *330mm f5.6 1/6 ISO250*

Tawny owl (Strix aluco) *75mm f8 1/250 ISO1600*

A different kind of photography, using flash to freeze the motion as the tawny owl lands on the post. Owls are a great subject to work with as they are very territorial and often hunt from favourite perches. This shot required two flash units set off camera in order to evenly light the subject as it prepared for landing.

Images that show the subject's characteristics or personality often make it stand out. This image shows how well camouflaged this tawny owl is against the trees in its natural habitat of the woodland.

Tawny owl (Strix aluco)   *500mm f4 1/800 ISO800*

Red deer (Cervus elaphus)

500mm f4 1/200 ISO5000

The 'magical sound' of the roaring of stags, the signature of the red deer rut. As the cuckoo is to spring, so the bellowing stag is to autumn and it says to the wildlife lover 'one of nature's great events' is in full swing.

Using golden colours of the autumn leaves adds to this lovely portrait of an owl.

I often think too late afterwards that I wish I had shot this image in both landscape and portrait. A valuable lesson; if a shot was worth taking one way, it was also worth taking the other way too, as shown with other subjects in this book.

Tawny owl (Strix aluco)   *500mm f4 1/800 ISO250*

Blue tit (Cyanistes caeruleus)   *500mm f4.5 1/1000 ISO1000*

Another project I commenced at home, setting up a feeding station and adding props. Focusing on local species over a period of time allows you to tell their story in depth as well as often learning new things about them. The resultant journey in this case is a creative rather than a physical one.

The long-eared owl can be found in many areas of Britain and Ireland, but it's not common and, being nocturnal, it's rarely seen. It prefers conifer woodlands (trees such as pine and spruce).

Long-eared owl (Asio otus)   *500mm f4 1/400 ISO1600*

1 2 3 4 5 6 7 8 9 10 11 12 13 14 15 16 17 18 19 20 21 22 23 24 25 26 27 **28** 29 30 31

Pheasant (Phasianus colchicus)   *400mm f5.6 1/6400 ISO800*

The pheasant is not native to Britain but has a long history of residence here. There is some debate over the success of various possible introductions dating back to the Romans, but it's generally agreed that pheasants were common in the UK by the 15th century.

Using the low key technique can create an image that is dark, moody and full of contrast. This image was taken at the moment the light picked out the subject whilst the background was still in the shade. To achieve this kind of shot, negative exposure compensation is used which helps to accentuate the feathers of the kingfisher against the dark background.

Kingfisher (Alcedo atthis)   *500mm f4 1/800 ISO125*

Rabbit (Oryctolagus cuniculus)   *500mm f4 1/800 ISO40*

An example of how the common subject shouldn't be overlooked. It should not always be about the rare or unusual, but often we ignore what is on our very doorstep which can make a lovely image, such as this rabbit. I often comment that I am not a snob when it comes to my subject, I am happy to work with anything that I can photograph well.

Another example of when to take a photo both portrait and landscape. As stated previously, if the image is worth taking one way, it may also be worth taking the other too, and the result gives a totally different image.

Goshawk (Accipiter gentilis)   *500mm f4 1/500 ISO3200*

Goshawk (Accipiter gentilis)

176mm f5 1/320 ISO3200

Goshawks (from the Old English for 'goose-hawk') are more likely to hunt hares, rabbits, squirrels, waterfowl, game-birds, corvids and pigeons. They will crash through vegetation in pursuit and even give chase on foot. This is what has made them one of the ultimate birds for falconers.

Another example of a blue tit perched on a seasonal branch. This kind of image can be achieved by strategically placing feeders close by, and sometimes birds will form a queue on the surrounding branches.

Blue tit (Cyanistes caeruleus)   *330mm f16 1/250 ISO500*

Knot (Calidris canutus), oystercatcher (Haematopus ostralegus)   *600mm f7.1 1/25 ISO3200*

An image of the flock of knot at Snettisham, Norfolk. Often termed the 'wader spectacular' at times of high tides around the Wash and all the migratory birds are forced to leave their feeding grounds on the mudflats and flock into the lagoons waiting for the tide to turn. This image shows how it can be difficult to separate an individual to focus on, unless it's a different species like this oystercatcher.

1 2 3 4 5 6 7 8 9 10 11 12 13 14 15 16 17 18 19 20 21 22 23 24 25 26 27 28 29 30   NOV

Knot (Calidris canutus)   *600mm f5.6 1/80 ISO800*

Known as the 'wader spectacular' during winter months, up to 50,000 knot gather around the Wash. During the high tides, these birds are forced off the mudflats by the fast incoming tide. They take off in one great throng, performing a spectacular dance in the sky, twisting and turning, a mass of swarming birds, before they settle further along the mudflats. This is repeated again and again, until they are finally defeated by the rising tide and fly over the sandbank to rest in the lagoon.

NOV   1 2 3 4 5 6 7 8 9 10 11 12 13 14 15 16 17 18 19 20 21 22 23 24 25 26 27 28 29 30

Grey seal (Halichoerus grypus)   *500mm f11 1/160 ISO800*

As stated previously photographs are about a moment in time but they can also be used to communicate feelings and emotions. This image shows a moment of tenderness between a pup and its mother as she returns from a fishing trip at sea to feed her young.

Otter (Lutra lutra)

500mm f5.6 1/1600 ISO1600

Certain light conditions can make an image appear very flat, lacking in colour or contrast. In these circumstances it can be beneficial to convert the image to black and white, such as with this otter.

Otter (Lutra lutra)

500mm f6.3 1/1600 ISO1600

Otters, one of my favourite subjects, but can also be one of the most challenging. Otters are very shy and to get close to one requires good fieldcraft and often luck. Any movement must be slow and whilst the otter is not looking your way, when it dives for example. You will also need to check the wind direction and keep downwind of it.

Eagle owl (Bubo bubo)

500mm f4.5 1/800 ISO400

There are estimated to be 12-40 pairs of eagle owls now nesting in Britain, however it's still uncertain how many of these escaped from captivity, and how many have immigrated here from Europe. Nobody has told the owls about Brexit obviously!

Snowy owl (Nyctea scandiaca)   *24mm f6.3 1/2500 ISO1250*

There are six species of owl that breed in the UK, plus the snowy owl. The snowy owl still appears in the UK, but has not been recorded as breeding here since the early seventies. This is a captive bird shot in the beautiful hills surrounding the Lake District.

A shot of the mighty eagle owl. These birds are one of the largest species of owl, and females can grow to a total length of 75 cm (30 in), with a wingspan of 188 cm (6 ft 2 in).

Eagle owl (Bubo bubo)   *500mm f5 1/4000 ISO800*

Harvest mouse (Micromys minutus)   *321mm f11 1/800 ISO3200*

This image to me screams autumn. With plentiful fruit to harvest, this busy mouse is making the most of it before the scarcity. An added value here are the autumnal colours of the trees in the background.

A beautiful barn owl shot as the sun sets. This image was taken while shooting against the light and into the sun. The soft feathers around the face, in particular, rim-lit by the last rays of the sun.

Barn owl (Tyto alba)   *500mm f5.6 1/1600 ISO1600*

Barn owl (Tyto alba)   *500mm f5.6 1/1600 ISO160€*

Another great example that if an image is worth capturing one way, it's often worth trying the other way too. As stated before it's noticeable how much larger the owl looks in the landscape shot compared to the portrait version.

The perfect reflection, this time using flash in the image to freeze the movement of the wings.

Great tit (Parus major)   *176mm f7.1 1/250 IS0640*

Avocet (Recurvirostra avosetta)   *500mm f6.3 1/1000 ISO200*

Large flocks of waders may gather during winter months as part of their annual migration. This increase in numbers can attract predators, such as the peregrine falcon. On occasion the predator sends the flocks into the air, where they group in order to try to confuse the predator and evade capture.

Another image working with a reflection pool and the local garden birds. This one uses a curved branch, forming an almost perfect circle with its reflection.

Blue tit (Cyanistes caeruleus)   *148mm f8 1/250 ISO800*

Great tit (Parus major)   *400mm f8 1/250 ISO200*

As with previous images, blurring the foreground and the background makes this great tit stand out, this time in a sea of yellow, which again complements the colour of the bird.

The use of the modern digital SLR's high frame rate, allows for several images of the same set-up to be taken, and enables you to choose the best pose. In this example, it was the image with the best wing position.

Blue tit (Cyanistes caeruleus)   *150mm f8 1/250 ISO200*

Common seal (Phoca vitulina)   *365mm f5.6 1/2000 ISO250*

This image of a common seal was taken whilst photographing grey seals during their breeding season. The common seals breed at a different time of the year, during the summer and therefore this seal was merely resting and not with a pup. Because of this I knew I had to approach this seal more carefully, using good fieldcraft and not rush in.

Grey seal (Halichoerus grypus) *500mm f4 1/3200 ISO1000*

In winter, the largest colony of grey seals breed around the Norfolk coastline at Blakeney Point. The seals arrive in November and have one thing on their mind, to procreate. The resulting pups are inquisitive and remind me of puppies, as they explore their surroundings, playing with pebbles and other objects they find on the beach.

Bittern (Botaurus stellaris)   *600mm f4 1/1600 ISO2000*

The winter time can be one of the best times to see these shy and elusive birds, as some of the vegetation may have been cut in areas of habitat management and water levels may also be higher.

Kestrel (Falco tinnunculus)   *300mm f7.1 1/2000 ISO800*

Kestrels have the ability to see in near ultraviolet light. They use it to track rodents that leave constant urine trails around their burrows. By the side of the road, the heavier emission vehicles make these trails even more visible. This is why so many kestrels hunt by the roadside, unfortunately all too often to their cost.

NOV 1 2 3 4 5 6 7 8 9 10 11 12 13 14 15 16 17 18 19 20 21 22 **23** 24 25 26 27 28 29 30

Barn owl (Tyto alba) *24mm f11 1/250 ISO1600*

An image of a barn owl hunting at night in a small meadow. This meadow was close to the owl's territory and so she often hunted here after dark. This was an image I had imagined for a while with both predator and prey in the frame. It has been suggested barn owls very rarely take moles, as they don't taste particularly nice. I have yet to try one, so I can't comment.

Red squirrel (Sciurus vulgaris)   *300mm f5.6 1/125 ISO800*

Red squirrels forage for nuts and chestnuts in the autumn to store for the winter months. It has been suggested a squirrel can tell whether a nut is fit to eat or not by its weight.

Coal tit (Parus ater)   *420mm f4.5 1/100 ISO800*

The coal tit's the smallest member of our tit family. It exists in all counties of the UK and Ireland with an estimated population of 600,000 pairs.

Grey seal (Halichoerus grypus)   *500mm f4 1/1250 ISO1000*

After a cold, clear night gives birth to a beautiful dawn, I get an opportunity for a shot I had wanted for years; a seal on the beach during sunrise. Norfolk has one of the largest grey seal populations and in total 40% of the world's population live around the UK shores.

Ptarmigan (Lagopus mutus)

500mm f4.5 1/500 ISO800

High up in the Cairngorms these magnificent birds are masters of camouflage, changing their colour to suit the season. In winter they turn completely white, except for a short black tail. If they change too early, before the snow arrives, it can leave them vulnerable to predators. In summer their brown and yellow plumage blends into the heather and lichen covered rocks.

1 2 3 4 5 6 7 8 9 10 11 12 13 14 15 16 17 18 19 20 21 22 23 24 25 26 27 **28** 29 30

NOV

Ptarmigan (Lagopus mutus)

500mm f4.5 1/800 ISO800

These birds are perfectly adapted for the cold. This shot shows how the feet are covered in feathers acting as snow shoes and allowing them to walk on even the softest snow. The feathers also help to prevent heat loss.

Grey seal (Halichoerus grypus)

400mm f7.1 1/500 ISO400

Another shot of a fluffy white grey seal pup. Seals have no tear ducts, so they continually produce tears to wash their eyes. I call this shot, 'A tear for wildlife' as to me it represents what we are currently doing to not just wildlife, but to our planet. In the quest for greater wealth and with an ever increasing population we are not looking after what we need the most, 'our home'.

1 2 3 4 5 6 7 8 9 10 11 12 13 14 15 16 17 18 19 20 21 22 23 24 25 26 27 28 29 30

NOV

Grey seal (Halichoerus grypus)

45mm f11 1/250 ISO400

The grey seals mate almost as soon as their pups have been born. However, the egg lays dormant for several months before it starts to grow and the pup is born almost a year later.

Grey seal (Halichoerus grypus) 235mm f7.1 1/200 ISO200

With so many female grey seals on the beach giving birth and feeding their pups, the males fight to patrol the most densely populated areas for the right to mate with these females. Fights between the males can often be violent with fur flying and blood drawn.

Grey seal (Halichoerus grypus)   *50mm f8 1/500 ISO400*

This seal I nicknamed the sand monster. Despite seeming cute and cuddly, they can become aggressive if threatened, or in order to defend their young. This female approached me as I laid on the beach, so I backed off to give her more space and allow her to relax.

Grey seal (Halichoerus grypus)   *500mm f5 1/800 ISO250*

This image shows where adverse weather conditions can add something unique to a photograph. In the UK recently we have experienced more frequent high winds. In this case, I decided to go to the beach, knowing the sand would be blowing along it. I attempted to show the movement against a seal pup caught in the sandstorm, whilst also highlighting the individual sand particles by having a reasonably high shutter speed.

1 2 3 4 5 6 7 8 9 10 11 12 13 14 15 16 17 18 19 20 21 22 23 24 25 26 27 28 29 30 31   DEC

This unusual pose was captured during a spot of preening, and was the result of waiting for the moment as the owl lifted its head for only a split second. I love the grumpy look on its face; maybe preening is not its favourite pastime.

Short-eared owl (Asio flammeus)   *600mm f4.5 1/640 ISO3200*

DEC   1 2 3 4 5 6 7 8 9 10 11 12 13 14 15 16 17 18 19 20 21 22 23 24 25 26 27 28 29 30 31

Barn owl (Tyto alba) *28mm f6.3 13secs ISO2000*

'The Owl and the Plough'. This is a local bird I have been working with for almost three years now. She has a ring on her leg from which I have been able to obtain all the details in the various photos taken. Submitting the details to the BTO (British Trust for Ornithology), I have learnt how old she is and where she came from. The BTO have gained valuable information on how far the young travel and how long they stay in a particular area. This information is always worth submitting if you ever find a ring on a bird, dead or alive.

1 2 3 4 5 6 7 8 9 10 11 12 13 14 15 16 17 18 19 20 21 22 23 24 25 26 27 28 29 30 31

DEC

Red squirrel (Sciurus vulgaris)   *500mm f4 1/500 ISO2000*

A red squirrel's tail has many uses, including; for balance, communication, to slow them down when jumping, as well as a snuggly warm blanket when it's cold such as in this image.

Robin (Erithacus rubecula)

200mm f10 1/250 ISO640

This robin was a particularly tame bird, as robins in the UK often can be. This made the shot easier to achieve, as the subject could be attracted to a specific area. Again flash has been used to freeze the motion.

1 2 3 4 5 6 7 8 9 10 11 12 13 14 15 16 17 18 19 20 21 22 23 24 25 26 27 28 29 30 31

DEC

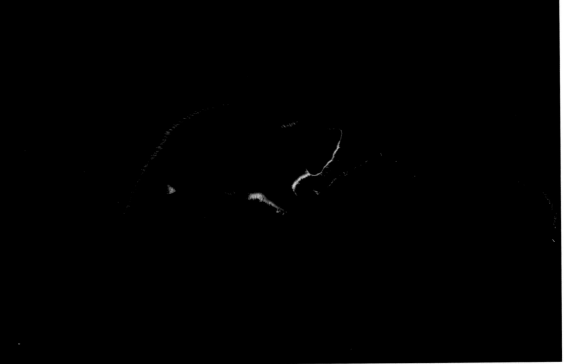

Pine marten (Martes martes)   *500mm f4 1/250 ISO3200*

This is another example of a backlit shot. This time placing the light source behind a pine marten and trying to achieve a rim-light around it. This can work well with subjects with fur, as the light shines through the hair making the shape identifiable.

Blue tit (Cyanistes caeruleus)

600mm f4 1/640 ISO3200

On a cold winter's morning, it can be worth making the effort to leave your cosy, warm bed, as a sharp frost doesn't always last that long and can disappear in only a few hours. A shot like this, with added interest can be your reward.

In winter mornings, you often have to wait for the sun to come up and provide enough light to make it worthwhile pressing the shutter. These next two images used LED lights to provide enough light to photograph as I was waiting for the sun to rise.

Water rail (Rallus aquaticus)   *500mm f4 1/60 ISO2000*

Little grebe (Tachybaptus ruficollis)   *500mm f4 1/50 ISO2000*

As in the opposite image, this little grebe swam towards the hide into the area lit with the artificial lights. Not to everyone's taste, but it does give the image a different quality.

Another reflection! This time a lovely red squirrel with handsome ear tufts. These tufts are present most of the year, but they do moult them out in the late summer and regrow them during the autumn. They are most prominent during winter months.

Red squirrel (Sciurus vulgaris)   *500mm f4.5 1/640 ISO1000*

Sparrowhawk (Accipiter nisus) 500mm f4.5 1/2000 ISO640

I always like to show behaviour in my shots, and this is one such example showing the male sparrowhawk mantling, to hide its prey, as the larger female was close by.

Red grouse (Lagopus lagopus scoticus)   *400mm f6.3 1/250 ISO200*

A red grouse shot in the Yorkshire Dales. During the breeding season, the males often wander close to the roadside first thing in the morning, before it gets too busy. However, they can be shot from the car at different times of the year too, it's just a matter of being lucky.

Otter (Lutra lutra)   *371mm f5.6 1/4000 ISO400*

I have often been out walking along river banks at first light. Sitting still for a few minutes, you'll be surprised what you may see, like this otter swimming so close that I could only fit its head in the frame.

Another example of natural framing, in this case using the tree to provide a border around the crested tit.

Crested tit (Lophophanes cristatus)   *500mm f4 1/250 ISO2500*

Robin (Erithacus rubecula)   *500mm f4 1/640 ISO1600*

Reflection pools can be a great way to photograph wildlife, particularly birds. In this case a river was used in an attempt to attract water species, and this opportunistic robin used the shallows to grab a free meal.

tter (Lutra lutra)

500mm f5.6 1/1250 ISO2500

A shot of a mother otter curled up with her cub on the seaweed shore. Many of my shots have suggested how the aim is to get as low as possible, and with otters this is certainly beneficial. However, this shot does also demonstrate the danger with getting low, as sometimes the foreground can obscure the subject.

Treecreeper (Certhia familiaris)

500mm f4 1/320 ISO3200

A treecreeper in the Highlands of Scotland. I had been busy photographing crested tits when this bird flew in and demanded to have its photo taken. It's great when the subjects come to you.

Grey seal (Halichoerus grypus)   *200mm f 6.3 1/6400 ISO800*

Silhouettes are a particular favourite of mine, however they only work with certain subjects. It requires the subject to be easily identifiable, with a distinctive shape. With seals it can be difficult to get low enough and still be able to shoot upwards to include the subject and the sky.

Sanderling (Calidris alba)   *600mm f6.3 1/5000 ISO1000*

This bird is in its winter plumage. They usually run along the beach at the waterline, avoiding the waves. This can make photographing them a wet affair if you misjudge the incoming waves yourself.

1 2 3 4 5 6 7 8 9 10 11 12 13 14 15 16 17 18 19 20 21 **22** 23 24 25 26 27 28 29 30 31

DEC

Crested tit (Lophophanes cristatus)

500mm f5.6 1/2500 ISO200

As stated earlier, silhouettes only work with certain subjects. This crested tit, with its distinctive shape, is one such example. There are so few birds with a crest, especially in the UK.

Waxwing (Bombycilla garrulus)

700mm f5.6 1/2500 ISO800

Another of my favourite birds. I used to think this was a mythical bird when I studied it in bird books as a kid. Since then I have been lucky enough to see some in real life - but still only a few, as they do not breed in the UK, but are a winter visitor. Some years they visit in larger numbers, called irruptions, when the population on its breeding grounds gets too large for the food available.

Another shot taken in my back garden, again showing that providing water and food can soon encourage a diverse range of wildlife to visit.

This robin nests in the ivy outside my back door, allowing me the opportunity to enjoy its busy life during the spring as it raises its new family.

Robin (Erithacus rubecula)   *500mm f5.6 1/800 ISO1600*

Grey seal (Halichoerus grypus) 125mm f4 1/800 ISO1000

Another example of a grey seal, but this time using a smaller lens in order to show the environment in which it's living, in this case, a sandy beach in Norfolk.

Red squirrel (Sciurus vulgaris)

500mm f5.6 1/1250 ISO2500

A shot showing the superb athleticism of the red squirrel, as it flies through the air. A shot like this is possible by pre-focusing on a point where you predict the subject will cross. Achieving a shot with the subject perfectly in focus, and in the right pose, can take some time.

DEC 1 2 3 4 5 6 7 8 9 10 11 12 13 14 15 16 17 18 19 20 21 22 23 24 25 26 27 28 29 30 31

Red squirrel (Sciurus vulgaris)   *300mm f4.5 1/4000 ISO3200*

A similar shot to the previous one, however a side-on view is slightly easier to achieve as the subject should remain on the same focal plane throughout its journey so at least it should always be in focus.

Mute swan (Cygnus olor)   *28mm f8 1/500 ISO3200*

A proper winter scene, with snow and frost masking the landscape. I have always wanted an image of a red deer in snow. On this particular trip to find some deer to photograph, I was sidetracked by the scene and the swans, and I spent the next three hours photographing them. By the time I had finished, the snow had melted hence the search for a shot of deer in the snow continues.

Great tit (Parus major)   *235mm f18 1/250 ISO1000*

This is a male great tit, which can be identified by the black stripe on its chest going all the way down its front to the tail.

Blue tit (Cyanistes caeruleus)

235mm f18 1/250 ISO1000

The blue tit's extremely irritable and persistent. Once it has decided what it wants it will not let itself be run off without a proper fight. This shot was achieved by using flash again, to freeze the action.